EASY COOKING FOR ONE OR TWO

Louise Davies left King's College of Household and Social Science (now King's College, London) with a B.Sc. degree and a conviction that scientists need interpreting. She has therefore combined the study of nutrition with writing, broadcasting, interviewing, lecturing and appearing on television. At the Ministry of Food she wrote a monthly magazine, *Food and Nutrition*, for dietitians and home economics teachers. Her first book, *See How to Cook*, was a pioneer amongst picture cookery books. For twelve years she broadcast *Shopping List* twice weekly in the BBC *Today* programme, giving advice on shopping and recipes, combining this and other broadcasts with a busy home life. Now, as head of the Gerontology Nutrition Unit at the Royal Free Hospital School of Medicine, she is conducting research into nutritional needs before and after the age of retirement from work and is actively encouraging practical help for those who shop for one or two, recipients of meals on wheels and residents in homes for elderly people. She gained a Ph.D. with the thesis 'Dietary Survey on a Group of Elderly People', later rewritten as a book, *Three Score Years . . . and Then!* (1981). The first edition of *Easy Cooking for One or Two* was published by Penguin in 1972 and was followed by *Easy Cooking for Three or More* (1975) and *More Easy Cooking for One or Two* (1979). In 1978 she was awarded an International Prize in Modern Nutrition. She has advised on osteoporosis and malnutrition of the elderly for the World Health Organisation and is deputy chairman of the International Union of Nutritional Sciences Committee on Geriatric Nutrition. Dr Davies is a widow with two daughters.

Louise Davies

Easy Cooking for One or Two

Illustrated by Tony Odell

PENGUIN BOOKS

For
My Daughters in the Kitchen
and My Son in the Law

PENGUIN BOOKS

Published by the Penguin Group
27 Wrights Lane, London W8 5TZ, England
Viking Penguin Inc., 40 West 23rd Street, New York, New York 10010, USA
Penguin Books Australia Ltd, Ringwood, Victoria, Australia
Penguin Books Canada Ltd, 2801 John Street, Markham, Ontario, Canada L3R 1B4
Penguin Books (NZ) Ltd, 182–190 Wairau Road, Auckland 10, New Zealand

Penguin Books Ltd, Registered Offices: Harmondsworth, Middlesex, England

First published 1972
Revised edition 1988
10 9 8 7 6 5 4 3

Filmset in Linotron Trump by
Rowland Phototypesetting Ltd
Bury St Edmunds, Suffolk
Printed and bound in Great Britain by
Cox & Wyman Ltd, Reading, Berkshire

Contents

List of Illustrations

Foreword

The plethora of dietary advice we are given these days is confusing for us all. The elderly – and indeed all people living on their own – are understandably anxious to maintain their independence, but many become weary with tedious and repetitive food preparation and over-elaborate recipes. Yet the ability to feed themselves – well – is vital to their independence. This new edition of a well-established handbook written especially for them takes this into account, allowing for a wide range of culinary expertise, so that recipes are included which are suitable for the physically handicapped cook as well as for the more active, eager to try more adventurous recipes.

SIR DONALD ACHESON
Chief Medical Officer, DHSS

Preface

It is fashionable to talk about an ageing population, to give statistics of the increasing proportion of people that now survive to become elderly or – to use one of the many euphemisms for old age – survive to become senior citizens. We talk, too, of social problems that arise, and especially we talk of their nutritional needs. Do they need the same amounts of calories and protein, of vitamins and minerals, as they did when they were younger, or do they need more, or perhaps less? What sorts of food should they be eating to get these nutrients? What are they in fact eating, and how far are they getting their requirements? And are there alternative foods that would suit them better, because they prefer them, or because they can prepare them more easily, or because they keep better?

Many of these questions continue to require rigid scientific study, for we still do not know all of the answers. It was to try to get some of these answers that in 1968 we set up in this Department the Gerontology Nutrition Unit under the leadership of Louise Davies. She and her colleagues have been finding out whether it is true that people's taste sensitivity and preferences change as they grow older, how they react to particular prepared foods that are already on the market, the extent to which the Meals on Wheels service satisfies their wants as well as their nutritional needs.

But Louise Davies is not content to look at these problems only as part of scientific research. She has taken a great interest in participating in, and initiating, cookery classes for the elderly. She has gained a great deal of experience in knowing what foods the elderly like, what sorts of dishes they can readily prepare, and more particularly how to combine both what they like and what they can make with the essential feature of high nutritional value at reasonable cost.

The recipes in this book show how well Dr Davies has succeeded in producing this combination of features. But she has done much more. The recipes include dishes that are simple to make for the man – or woman – who has had little experience in cooking, but they also include more ambitious dishes that will appeal to the experienced or venturesome. They contain several suggestions for novel dishes, or novel ways of preparing old favourites, so as to help overcome the tendency of lonely, elderly people gradually to lose interest in food because they are eating a monotonous and often badly balanced diet. The recipes have also, every one of them, been tested not only for practicality, but for acceptability by the sort of people for whom they are designed. They are by no means just the same sort of recipes as those you will find in standard cook books simply scaled down to make a meal for one or two.

I am certain that this book will go a long way towards helping to overcome some of the more difficult problems that face elderly people.

JOHN YUDKIN
Emeritus Professor,
Queen Elizabeth College

Preface to Revised Edition

When *Easy Cooking for One or Two* was first published, I was sure that it would be welcomed by those who were looking for simple, tasty recipes that would also ensure good nutrition. The fact that, since then, the publishers have had to reprint the book nearly twenty times confirms my original assessment. I can do no better than repeat precisely what I wrote in 1972 and to predict a similar success for the new updated edition.

JOHN YUDKIN
Emeritus Professor of Nutrition
University of London

Acknowledgements

Professor John Yudkin and Professor Arnold E. Bender, at Queen Elizabeth College, and Dr Bruce MacGillivray, at the Royal Free Hospital School of Medicine, have given active encouragement to the work of the Gerontology Nutrition Unit and have helped me by discussing the nutritional details in this book.

My thanks to Ruth Golding, Home Economist, and Sue Thomas, Dietitian, for their invaluable help with the testing of these recipes; also to Jeannette Grant who helped to test recipes for the first edition, many of which are retained in this revision. Several of Patricia Coleman's Canadian dishes (from our previous collaboration) have become firm favourites of mine and have also been included.

I am grateful to Paula Wood for practical advice, and to Home Economist colleagues at British Meat, the Flour Advisory Bureau, the National Dairy Council, the Seafish Industry Authority and Van den Berghs. Recipes from the Cookery Classes are acknowledged in Chapter 4. A heartfelt thank you to Marion Heber for her speedy, accurate typing, and to Helen Edwardson and Kathleen McCooke who cheerfully helped me to clear up the chaos from the test cooking.

With great appreciation may I record that during the past few years the work of the Gerontology Nutrition Unit has been made possible by generous donations from charitable trusts and:

The National Dairy Council of England and Wales, in association with the E E C in Brussels

John Lewis Partnership

Marks & Spencer

J. Sainsbury plc (Sainsbury's)

The Ministry of Agriculture, Fisheries and Food

Chapter 1

Nutrition on Your Own

When you are on your own
- quantities for one can be difficult to find; often you are obliged to buy too much, so left-over food has to be thrown out;
- food costs and fuel bills can be proportionately higher;
- loneliness may make you lose your appetite; or it may have the opposite effect because some people tend to eat too many readily available fattening fillers when they are feeling lonely;
- you may not feel like bothering to cook for yourself.

For all these reasons, and more, your diet – and your health – may suffer.

For those living on their own there are three basic rules for better eating:

1. EAT SOMETHING OF EVERYTHING, AND NOT TOO MUCH OF ANY ONE THING. Do not narrow your diet unless directed to do so by a doctor or dietitian. The nourishment your body needs is spread through many different foods, so avoid monotony.

2. THERE IS NO FOOD THAT YOU MUST HAVE. Do not listen to the know-it-alls who insist that you must eat 'raw carrots' or 'liver once a week'. Certainly these foods are good for you, but millions live for more than three-score years and ten without them. If you positively dislike a certain food, there are always equally nourishing alternatives.

3. SOME FOODS ARE BETTER FOR YOU THAN OTHERS.
As a nation we are being advised that we should avoid the
high-fat, high-sugar and high-salt items, and alcohol in
excess. Yet these are among the purchases most tempt-
ingly advertised. Eating and drinking them may seem the
most desirable way to satisfy your hunger or thirst, but we
are being warned that they can be connected with our high
incidence of coronary heart disease, dental caries and
overweight. The recipes in this book have been updated to
include an even wider choice of the foods that are 'better
for you', such as fruits and vegetables, cereals and breads.

If you have been advised to take especial care, you can
easily make substitutions in many of our recipes. For
instance, instead of whole milk you could substitute
skimmed or semi-skimmed; you could choose low-fat
varieties of cheese and yogurt, leaner meats, less butter or
margarine, brown or wholemeal bread or flour rather than
white; herbs and lemon juice in place of salt . . .

*However, although we are delighted that our recipes
are being used by people of all ages who are cooking for
one or two, they are particularly designed for those past
retirement age. Fortunately, one of the delights of growing
older is that by the time you pass your mid-seventies
many dietary risks are reduced. After that stage it is more
important to ask yourself these questions:*

Are You Eating Too Little?

In countries where there is an ample supply of food, it is
unusual for anyone to starve. But there are times when
you may need to take extra nourishment, for example
● when there has been a period of going without food
  (possibly through incapacity, bereavement or loneliness

in old age) and more flesh needs to be put back on wasted bodies;

- especially during convalescence;
- when nourishing foods have been avoided because of price;
- when nourishing foods have been avoided because they are difficult to chew;
- when you are constipated or have an illness such as diverticulitis and your food is too low in dietary fibre;
- when there is a danger of hypothermia in cold weather (food – hot or cold – keeps up the internal temperature of the body).

It is at these times that you may feel least like bothering to cook. So, to make sure you are not neglecting your diet, we list below a few examples from the recipes in this book that you could prepare for yourself or have cooked for you:

Are You Eating Too Much?

Eating too much for your energy requirements can become a habit, and this habit can start you on the road to obesity.

But it is more difficult to lose weight when you are old than when you are young, and many doctors feel that the effort of following 'slimming diets' by their elderly patients is generally not worthwhile in results.

Nevertheless, you cannot be at your healthiest if you are very overweight. Even walking and shopping become more tiring. If you fall, you fall more heavily. If you have an illness, such as arthritis, or heart or bone trouble, extra weight makes it worse. Surgery or nursing can become a problem.

So what is the positive advice? If you need to lose weight, do not make the mistake of missing out meals. It is best to eat frequently, but make them *small* meals. Avoid excessive intake of alcohol and cut down on the high-sugar and high-fat items. Increase your physical activity as much as possible. These simple guidelines should also help to protect you from further weight gains.

Are You Eating With Friends?

For most of us, food preparation and eating are social occupations. A tight budget is seldom the main cause of malnutrition – a marked lack of interest in food is far more dangerous. So in this book we have included some dishes – such as Fresh Fruit Salad, Coleslaw 'Make-ahead' – that perk up appetite and are ideal to take with you when you visit solitary friends or relations.

The recipes in the chapter 'Favourites from the Cookery Classes' were enjoyed all the more because they were eaten in congenial company. But even some of the recipes in Chapter 2, 'Recipes for Non-Cooks', are suitable for entertaining: when friends visit, you could make a meal for them with a minimum of fuss.

An occasional meal eaten with friends may be looked forward to and need not overcommit you.

Are You Including High-fibre Foods?

Dietary fibre in foods can help to avoid constipation and to ease diverticulitis and similar problems.

Instead of bran supplements, or laxatives, you could eat more of the high-fibre foods now readily available in the shops: wholemeal breads and biscuits, high-fibre breakfast cereals (with milk for added calcium), brown rice and pasta, fresh, frozen, canned or dried peas, beans and lentils, and a wide range of fruits and vegetables.

If you do not fancy these, you can still get the benefit of a wide variety of dietary fibre by eating more potatoes, brown or white bread (if you prefer these to wholemeal or granary) and plenty of your favourite vegetables and fruits, including dried fruits.

When increasing dietary fibre it is important to have

enough fluid in your diet to enable the fibre to act efficiently.

Are You Drinking Enough Fluid?

Fluids – liquids of any kind, e.g., soup, tea, coffee, fruit juices – are essential throughout each day. They save us from dehydration, with its consequent first symptoms of headache, irritability and confusion. (If you have a mild headache, the water with which you take the aspirin may be just as effective as the aspirin itself!)

Sometimes, with age, the sensation of thirst is dulled. It is therefore especially important, once you have reached retirement age, to get into a habit of taking regular breaks for cups of tea or some other beverage. If you are anxious about getting up in the night, still drink plenty of fluids but take your beverages earlier in the day, not just before bedtime.

The water in foods also helps to avoid dehydration, but unfortunately alcoholic drinks have the opposite effect: alcohol actually leads to dehydration. So it is *non-*alcoholic beverages your body needs.

Alcohol in moderation can be good for you, although it is sometimes advised that you should give your system a rest and not take it every day of the week. For some medical conditions, the doctor will tell you that alcohol should be avoided altogether. You may be warned against alcoholic drinks if you are taking regular medication or short term treatment with drugs such as antibiotics. It is also advisable to avoid alcohol if a 'wee drop' makes you wake confused: it is easy to fall and injure yourself.

Are You Getting Fresh Air and Exercise?

A pleasant walk in the open air helps to stimulate the appetite and the mind. If you feel you lack the necessary stamina, a memorable piece of advice on walking is 'keep going; if you could do it yesterday, you can do it tomorrow!' It doesn't matter if your pace is slow: persevere!

The best advice at all ages is to be as healthily active as you can.

For most of us, activities such as a brisk daily walk, gardening, dancing, swimming or other sports are a good health insurance as we get older.

Even if you are immobilized through illness, keep moving as much as possible; sitting in a rocking chair is better than lying down on a sofa or bed to rest. Even if you are confined to a wheelchair, enquire about exercises you can do.

Moderate exercise is a simple prescription for health and it is of prime importance that no one should be housebound through a fear of venturing out of doors.

Are You Over-stressed?

Stress, unhappiness and fear not only affect your peace of mind, they can also severely disturb your digestive system. You can help yourself by remembering to

- sit up straight, not hunched, when you eat;
- chew food deliberately and slowly, so that you do not rush your meal or bolt your food;
- prepare the table or tray carefully avoiding the need to fuss up and down to fetch forgotten items;
- choose recipes to match your mood: the 'non-cooks' chapter in this book gives ideas for times when you need to keep well with the minimum of cooking effort;

subsequent chapters contain progressively more adventurous recipes; the 'store-cupboard' chapter can save you the bother of having to go out shopping.

Are You in a Muddle over Medicines and Mealtimes?

If you are taking medical drugs of any kind, do you know *exactly* when to take them in relation to your meals? Should they be taken between meals (i.e., on an empty stomach), just before a meal, during the meal (with the food) or after the meal on a full stomach? Ask your doctor or pharmacist.

Are You Relying on Nutritional Supplements?

The over-sixties have now become a potentially profitable market. So just beware of food cranks or self-appointed gurus who tell you that you need their 'little bottles'! If what they say is true ask yourself instead, 'Then what is wrong – and what needs to be put right – with my present food or lifestyle?'

All the essential nutrients come in the form of *foods*. So the aim of this book is to help you to eat and enjoy a nourishing diet. Once you do that it could be quite unnecessary and expensive to go to the chemist, health food shop or any other shop or mail order firm for health in the form of pills and potions, unless you are specifically advised to do so by your doctor. However, the question is often asked: How do I know that my diet is adequate? If this question worries you, for an 'insurance policy', you could take a multiple vitamin and mineral nutritional supplement just to top up your diet. Two or three times a week should be sufficient – don't overdo it. But I am of the firm opinion that food is more enjoyable than supplements!

A choice of foods particularly valuable for vitamins and minerals is given on page 258. If just now you would rather eat than read, turn to the recipes. They have all been chosen to be especially nourishing, but our panel of testers has made sure that, first and foremost, they are tempting to eat and easy to buy and prepare.

Chapter 2

Recipes for Non-cooks

The recipes in this chapter, as in all the other chapters, are arranged under subject headings, to help you to find them with ease. Also, see the Index, pages 269–279.

Contents

This chapter is for the times when you do not feel like cooking. It is also for those of you who have never had to cook and are now having to manage on your own. The recipes need scarcely any effort but they are nourishing as well as tempting.

There are a number of more adventurous recipes in the other chapters. You should find them easy to cook. Here are some examples and you may like to look for others:

Hot meals are satisfying and enjoyable and most people aim to have at least one cooked meal a day. However it is quite possible to be well nourished without this. It is not true that you can keep warm in winter only by eating hot food. Certainly, hot food is more inviting in cold weather but your body can keep warm from any nourishing food, hot or cold. If you feel you cannot face the chore of cooking, you may be tempted by ready-prepared nourishing cold snacks. Look for the sliced meats, ready-prepared salads, pickled herrings, smoked cod's roe, cheeses, scotch eggs, meat pies, yogurts, milk desserts and similar foods. It is better to have these and relax than to force yourself to cook when you do not feel like it.

Lazy Soup

Comment from Arbroath, Angus Cookery Class: 'We thought it easy and nourishing and a nice change.'

Serves 1
Cooking time: only a few minutes

INGREDIENTS

1 scant cup of water
1 teaspoon Marmite
or 1 teaspoon Bovril

or ½ chicken stock cube
1 egg, size 4 or 5

METHOD

1   In a small pan, bring the water to the boil.
2   Stir in the Marmite, or Bovril, or the chicken stock cube and dissolve it. Leave over low heat.
3   Beat the egg well with a fork in a small jug or cup.
4   Lift the jug or cup well above the soup and pour in a thin trickle. Do not stir.
    The egg sets in a soft thick 'vermicelli'.
5   Serve immediately before the egg has time to set hard.

Savoury Milk

A comforting drink for elevenses or a nightcap.

The version using the chicken stock cube can be served as a milky chicken soup for lunch.

INGREDIENTS

a cup of hot milk
1 level teaspoon Bovril or
   Marmite

or ½ chicken stock cube

METHOD

Stir the Bovril, Marmite or chicken stock cube into the very hot milk until it dissolves.

Tomato Soup and Egg

Serves 2

INGREDIENTS

1 small can ready-to-serve
   cream of tomato soup

a little milk (optional)
1 hard-boiled egg

METHOD

1   Hard boil the egg – or see Coddled Eggs (hard) on page 24.
2   Heat the tomato soup, with or without a little added milk.
3   Serve the soup with half a hard-boiled egg in each soup plate. Eat with a spoon, chopping the egg into small pieces.

Light Mayonnaise Dressing

If you find shop-bought mayonnaise too oily or rich, lighten it with low-fat plain yogurt.

INGREDIENTS

low-fat plain yogurt
mayonnaise

METHOD

1   To every spoonful of mayonnaise, stir in a spoonful of plain yogurt.

Tomato Sauce (Quick Method)

INGREDIENTS

half a 1-pint packet tomato
   soup mix
8 fluid oz. (1 teacup) of water
1 tomato (chopped)
½ teaspoon Marmite

METHOD

1   In a small pan mix everything together and, con-
    tinuously stirring, heat until boiling.
2   Simmer for 5 minutes, with occasional stirring.

Note: It is not necessary to skin the tomato, unless you
prefer. Serve with meat, fish, hot pies or MUSHROOM AND
BACON ROLY POLY, page 176.

Nourishing Cereal

Serves 1

INGREDIENTS

1 egg
½ cup of cold milk
1 teaspoon to 1 dessertspoon
vitamin C blackcurrant
drink

portion of cornflakes, bran
flakes or other favourite
cereal

METHOD

1 With a fork beat the egg in a cup.
2 Add the milk (to save using another cup to measure, reckon that the egg plus half a cup of milk almost fills a normal-sized cup).
3 Stir in the blackcurrant (amount according to taste).
4 Strain over the cereal to remove the thread of egg white and serve.

Note: There is no flavour of raw egg in this dish – it just makes a pleasantly rich, creamy milk.

Quick alternative: For another nourishing cereal, just add cut-up banana and a few raisins to muesli or other cereal and milk.

Croque Monsieur

This hot sandwich with a difference is simply a cheese and ham sandwich dipped in egg and milk before frying. It makes a satisfying meal when served with tomatoes or a salad. Delicious, but not for those watching their fat intake!

Serves 2

INGREDIENTS

4 slices brown bread, lightly
  buttered
2 slices ham
2 oz. Cheddar cheese, sliced
1 egg, size 4 or 5

3 tablespoons milk
salt and pepper
a little butter or margarine
  for frying

METHOD

1   Make sandwiches of the ham and cheese by layering one on top of the other in the buttered bread.
2   Whisk together the egg and milk and add a little seasoning. Dip the sandwiches into this mixture, turning to soak both sides.
3   Heat the fat in a frying pan until just beginning to turn brown then use to fry the sandwiches on both sides. Serve immediately.

Cheese and Ketchup Toasted Sandwich or Cheese and Ham Toasted Sandwich

An ordinary cheese sandwich is a nourishing snack. But a hot toasted sandwich makes a more satisfying, tempting meal.

Serves 1
Cooking time: approximately 8 minutes

INGREDIENTS

a little butter or margarine
2 slices of bread

tomato ketchup, or your
    favourite chutney or
    pickle
1 oz. Cheddar cheese, sliced

METHOD

1   Spread the bread with tomato ketchup.
2   Place cheese in the middle to make an unbuttered sandwich at this stage.
3   Now spread the outsides of the sandwich with butter or margarine.
4   Place on grill-grid and grill each side till golden brown, using your knife and fork for turning. Serve piping hot.

For Cheese and Ham as an Alternative Filling

1   Spread the bread with a little made mustard instead of tomato ketchup.
2   Top with slices of Cheddar cheese and a slice of ham.
3   Make the sandwich as above, then grill each side until golden brown.

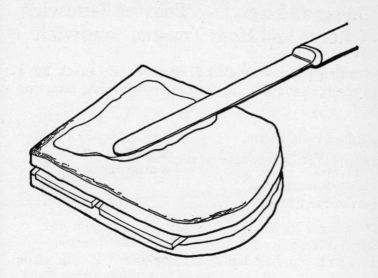

Other Ideas for Toasted Sandwiches

(For thick or juicy fillings it is best to use an electric sandwich toaster which seals the edges of the bread.)

Savoury
Baked beans and cooked
  sausage
Cheese and apple
Cheese, bacon and
  mushroom
Cheese, tomato and
  mushroom
Corned beef and tomato
Egg and sardine
Ham and pineapple
Scrambled egg and bacon
Tuna and tomato

Sweet
Apple and sultana
Banana, raisin and
  cinnamon
Pear and ginger marmalade

Cheese 'Pizza'

Serves 1–2
Cooking time: approximately 10 minutes

INGREDIENTS

2 rashers streaky bacon
   (rinds removed, rashers
   cut into 3)
1 bap or soft bread roll
   (wholemeal or white)

2 oz. Cheddar cheese (sliced
   and crumbled)
1 tomato (sliced)

METHOD

1   Cut bap in half across, topping each half with bacon, and grill gently until bacon is cooked and bap lightly browned – about 5–6 minutes.
2   Place cheese and tomato on top of bacon and grill lightly until cheese just begins to melt.

Toasted Cheese

Serves 1
Cooking time: about 5 minutes

INGREDIENTS

1 medium-thick slice of   Cheddar cheese
   bread

METHOD

1   Toast the bread on one side under the grill.
2   Slice the cheese thinly and put, slightly overlapping,
     over the entire surface of the untoasted side of the
     bread.
3   Toast the cheese until it melts and begins to bubble
     and brown. Do not overcook. Serve at once.

Note: For added flavour, spread a little pickle, chutney or
tomato ketchup on the bread under the cheese before
toasting.

Coddled Eggs – Foolproof Method

How many times have you heard 'she can't even boil an egg'? But boiling an egg is not a job any fool can do, unless one is clever enough to use the foolproof method. Our method is more correctly called 'coddling' because the egg, though tasting like a boiled egg, is not actually boiled for more than a few seconds, but is merely left in very hot water.

Coddled Eggs (soft)

1   If the eggs are kept in a refrigerator it is best to allow them to regain room temperature by taking them out of the fridge 2 to 3 hours, at least, before using.
2   In a small pan bring water to the boil. It must be a fast rolling boil. The quantity must be enough to cover the eggs when they are put in.
3   Using a spoon, lower the eggs into the water.
4   Turn out the heat, immediately cover the pan and remove from the heat.
5   Allow to stand for 8 minutes.

Coddled Eggs (hard)

1   Remove eggs from refrigerator as before.
2   Place the eggs in a pan of cold water, covering them with at least a quarter of an inch of water.
3   Bring to the boil over medium to fast heat.

4 Turn out the heat, immediately cover the pan and remove from the heat.
5 Allow to stand for 15 minutes.
6 Take out the eggs and immediately plunge them into cold (preferably running) water to stop them cooking further and producing the unappetizing black ring which appears between white and yolk when eggs are overcooked.

Egg and Onion

Serves 1

INGREDIENTS

1 small onion
a knob of butter or
    margarine

2 eggs, size 3 or 4
salt and pepper

METHOD

1 Peel and slice onion fairly thinly.
2 Fry in butter or margarine until softened but not browned.
3 Beat the eggs well with a fork or whisk and add seasoning to taste.
4 Pour the eggs on to onions and stir until scrambled.
5 Serve immediately.

This was my mother-in-law's favourite weekend supper snack. With it she served buttered water-biscuits, as a change from toast.

Mumbled Eggs

Serves 1
Cooking time: 2 or 3 minutes

This is an old-fashioned British recipe, popular in the days when our ancestors had longer, larger and more relaxed breakfasts than we do today. Mumbled eggs could have been just one of a whole series of dishes from which the well-to-do family helped themselves.

I am told that 'mumbled' means they are easy to eat, even if you have no teeth. This recipe is ideal for the beginner in cookery or anyone in a hurry, because there is not much washing up, especially if you use a flameproof oven-to-table pan.

INGREDIENTS

a knob of butter or
 margarine

2 eggs, size 3 or 4
salt and pepper

Serve with toast, bread and butter, water-biscuit or crispbread.

METHOD

1   Melt the butter or margarine in a pan.
2   Just break the fresh eggs into the fat without bothering to beat them first.
3   Add a generous pinch of salt and a sprinkle of pepper.
4   Stir vigorously with a fork till just set lightly. Remove from the heat when they are still slightly too liquid to eat: the warmth of the pan will finish cooking them.

Portuguese Egg

Serves 1
Cooking time: 5–10 minutes

INGREDIENTS

a knob of butter or
   margarine
4 oz. frozen peas*
1 tablespoon water*

salt and pepper
pinch of dried mixed herbs
1 egg
a slice of buttered toast

* A small can of garden peas, with its liquor, can be used
instead of the frozen peas and water.

METHOD

1   Put the butter or margarine, peas, water, seasoning and
herbs into a small flameproof dish. Set on a medium
heat until it begins to bubble.
2   Break the egg on to the surface, reduce the heat, cover
and cook until the egg sets.
3   Serve with hot buttered toast.

Kippers

To avoid cooking smells, one of the best ways to cook kippers is to place the kipper or kipper fillets in a jug or shallow dish and pour boiling water over them. Cover the jug or dish with a lid, a plate or with foil. Leave without further heating for 5 minutes. Drain off the water and you will find the kippers cooked to perfection.

Note: You may prefer to buy boil-in-the-bag kippers but sometimes a packet of kipper fillets or a large kipper is too much for one meal. Any left-overs can be flaked, kept cool and covered, and used the next day for kipper scramble.

Kipper Scramble

Serves 1

INGREDIENTS

1 kipper fillet
2 eggs, size 4
pepper

a knob of butter or
   margarine
a slice of buttered toast

METHOD

1   After cooking the kipper remove the skin and flake the fish whilst it is warm.
2   Beat the eggs, season with pepper but not salt, and add flaked kipper.
3   Melt knob of butter in a saucepan, pour in the egg mixture. Keep the heat low.
4   Stir continuously until the eggs are creamy and soft. Remove from the heat just before the mixture looks fully set as cooking continues in the heat of the pan.
5   Serve at once on buttered toast.

Scrambled Haddock and Eggs

If you have some smoked haddock left over after a meal, flake the left-over fish free from bones and keep – *cool and covered* – till next day.

If you are starting with a piece of raw smoked haddock, put it in a pan, just cover it with water, bring to the boil and simmer very gently for a minute or two. Then flake it free from bones.

Serves 1

INGREDIENTS

a knob of butter or
    margarine
a little flaked, cooked,
    smoked haddock

2 tablespoons milk
2 eggs, size 4

Serve with hot buttered toast.

METHOD

1   Melt the butter or margarine in a small pan. Put the flaked, smoked fish with the milk into the pan and bring to the boil.
2   Break in two eggs and stir vigorously with a wooden spoon until just before mixture looks fully set, as cooking continues in the heat of the pan.

Green Vegetables – Quick and Nourishing

1. WASH AND PREPARE ONLY JUST BEFORE USE.

- *Brussels sprouts* are best trimmed of outer, discoloured leaves, then cut down in half. This enables you to see whether they are clean right through, and also cuts down the cooking time because half sprouts cook through more quickly than whole sprouts. Wash them well in salted cold water before cooking.

- *Cabbage* should be shredded with a sharp knife and washed just before cooking. Shredded cabbage cooks more quickly than cabbage merely cut in halves or quarters.

- *Cauliflower* should be cleaned carefully in salted water, particular attention being paid to the base of the stems where dirt collects. Cut a cross in the bottom stem, after trimming it, to allow the heat to penetrate through the stem more quickly. Alternatively, for speedier cooking, break the cauliflower into small florets and cook with the leaves cut in short pieces.

- *Greens* should be washed and torn into rough pieces just before cooking.

2. COOK IN THE *MINIMUM* OF FAST-BOILING, VERY LIGHTLY SALTED WATER, WITH THE LID TIGHTLY ON THE PAN SO THAT THE VEGETABLES ARE MOSTLY COOKING IN STEAM.

If you use too much water (an inch in the pan is generally sufficient) valuable vitamin C can escape.

Whole cauliflowers need more water (a pan half filled with boiling water once the vegetable is in). To keep the flower white, place the flower-side down for the first five minutes then turn stem-side down till cooked (about 20 minutes in all).

Cauliflower florets and the other vegetables listed are generally just-cooked in 5 minutes.

3. SERVE IMMEDIATELY. Keeping vegetables warm also destroys vitamin C.

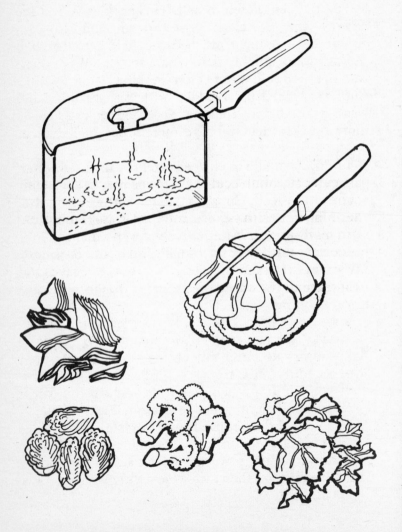

Cucumber and Yogurt

A refreshing salad, particularly good as a cold accompaniment for hot curry.

Serves 2–3

INGREDIENTS

½ unpeeled cucumber
salt

1 small carton of plain
  yogurt
chopped mint (optional)

METHOD

1 Slice the cucumber and cut across to make small cubes.
2 Sprinkle well with salt and leave for 10 to 15 minutes.
3 Rinse salt off with water and drain well.
4 Spoon the cucumber into its dressing of plain yogurt. When fresh mint is available, chop up a few leaves and stir them into the dressing.

Tomato Cups

A quickly prepared snack; or an easy first course for entertaining friends. Make it into a meal by serving with ready-cooked smoked mackerel fillet.

Serves 1–2

INGREDIENTS

1 medium to large tomato
canned mixed vegetables,
   drained*

home-made mayonnaise (or
   its nearest shop-bought
   equivalent)*

*   You may prefer to use a can of Russian Salad – this is a stronger flavoured mixture of vegetables in salad dressing.

METHOD

1   Cut the tomato across in halves, and with a sharp spoon scoop out and discard the pips.
2   Chop up the fleshy cross between the pips and stir with a few teaspoons of canned mixed vegetables.
3   Mix with mayonnaise and fill into the two tomato cups.

Tomato Slices

Serves 1

INGREDIENTS

2 small tomatoes
granulated sugar
olive oil

parsley, cress, spring onions
or dried basil

Serve as a 'starter' with crusty or wholemeal bread, or as a main meal with sliced ham, tongue or corned beef.

METHOD

1   With a serrated knife, cut the tomatoes across in slices. Arrange on plate.
2   Sprinkle with a good pinch of sugar.
3   Moisten with a quarter of a teaspoon, or less, of olive oil. Decorate with parsley, cress or spring onions snipped with scissors; if fresh 'greenery' is not available, sprinkle with dried basil.

Lemon Curd Spread

INGREDIENTS

1 small can condensed milk   rind and juice of a lemon
1 yolk of egg

METHOD

1   Beat all ingredients together.
2   Leave for two hours to thicken before using as a spread
    on bread and butter, or as a cake filling.

Notes: This is an easy method of making lemon curd with
a delicious home-made flavour.
    To use up the egg white, whip it into a fruit jelly on the
point of setting – this makes a light easy dessert.

Banana and Orange Yogurt

Serves 2

In just over 5 minutes you can make one of the most nourishing of desserts – equally tempting for an invalid or for entertaining guests.

INGREDIENTS

½ teacup (4 fluid oz.) orange juice*
1½ teaspoons gelatine
1 small pot mandarin orange yogurt

2 small bananas, peeled and sliced
whipping cream, or grated chocolate (optional)

* Use freshly squeezed or carton orange juice.

METHOD

1   Heat 3 tablespoons of the orange juice in a cup placed in a saucepan of simmering water. When hot remove from the pan, sprinkle in the gelatine and stir to dissolve. Cool for 2 or 3 minutes.
2   In a bowl, beat the rest of the orange juice with the yogurt (if you use a flat whisk this is smooth in a few seconds). Beat in the gelatine mixture.
3   Stir in the banana slices and transfer to serving dishes to cool and set. For 'swank' it can be decorated with a whirl of cream or a grating of chocolate.

Spiced Grapefruit

Serves 1
Oven temperature: 400°F, 200°C, gas mark 6 *or* cook under a hot grill
Cooking time: 8–10 minutes in oven, or about 5 minutes under grill

INGREDIENTS

½ grapefruit
1 tablespoon brown sugar (flat or heaped according to taste)

a generous pinch of mixed spice
a little margarine (less than ½ oz.)
1 glacé cherry (optional)

Serve hot with a cherry in the centre.

METHOD

1   Loosen the grapefruit from its skin and cut into segments leaving them in the skin.
2   Sprinkle with brown sugar and mixed spice.
3   Dot with small knobs of margarine.
4   Cook in pre-heated oven 400°F, 200°C, gas mark 6 for 8–10 minutes or under a hot grill for about 5 minutes.

Yogurt Jelly

Even if you do not fancy yogurt, try this jelly: it tastes like an extra-special milk jelly.

Serves 2–3 – keeps well from one day to the next

INGREDIENTS

½ packet of jelly, your own choice of flavour
boiling water

a 5-oz. carton plain yogurt (or, better still, a flavoured or fruit yogurt to match the flavour of the jelly)

METHOD

1   Place the jelly cubes in a heatproof measuring jug and pour on the boiling water up to the half-pint mark. Stir until dissolved.
2   Leave until cool, but not completely set. Add the yogurt, whisking it in or stirring it briskly with a fork, until it is all blended.
3   Pour into a dish, or separate dishes, and leave to set. This jelly is not quite stiff enough to turn out.

'Afternoon Nap' Tea

This is invaluable for those who are bed-ridden – the tray
can be prepared for them in advance. For those who just
feel tired, put this at the ready before you take a nap. It is
then not necessary to go and put the kettle on when you
wake up, just pop the tea-bag into the flask.

You need a half-pint vacuum flask.

Serves 1

1   Take a tray with a half-pint vacuum flask almost filled
    with boiling water.

2 Also put on the tray one tea-bag, milk and sugar (if liked), cup, saucer and spoon.
3 When required, drop the tea-bag in the flask, and allow 3–5 minutes' infusion, with cap replaced. (You may be surprised to find that it does not matter that the water is not 'on the boil' when the tea is made, but this vacuum-flask method is only suitable for tea-bags otherwise you will get floating tea-leaves.)
4 Pour yourself a cup of tea to your liking. (If you prefer, the water can be used to make a cup of coffee, using instant coffee in the cup or a coffee bag in the flask.)

Important note for winter: Preparing a tray like this, with a hot drink at the ready, can help to lessen the risk of hypothermia (a drop in inner body temperature). A well-insulated flask will keep the water hot for many hours.

Add biscuits or a sandwich (wrapped to keep it fresh) to the tray to give food as well as beverage – even though the food is cold it helps to keep the body warm.

Tea Grog

Serves 1

INGREDIENTS

boiling water
tea or 1 tea-bag
2 teaspoons rum

1 teaspoon sugar, or to taste
1 good slice lemon, or 1
   teaspoon pure lemon juice

METHOD

1   Make the tea in the usual way in a covered teapot,
allow three minutes' infusion. (It is best not to make
this tea too strong.)
   When you warm the teapot, warm a half-pint drinking glass* or mug with hot water at the same time and
empty just before required.
2   Put all the ingredients into the glass, fill up with tea
and stir.

Note: If you prefer to avoid alcohol, double the amount of
lemon for a deliciously refreshing LEMON TEA (especially
thirst-quenching in summer).

* Use a Pyrex 'drink-up' or some similar strong glass in a
holder.

Apple Juice Eggnog

Serves 2

INGREDIENTS

1 egg
¾ cup chilled apple juice

¼ cup cold skimmed milk
1 teaspoon honey
¼ teaspoon cinnamon

METHOD

1   Combine all the ingredients in a bowl or blender.
2   Whisk or blend until frothy. Serve at once.

Note: The apple and milk may look curdled, but this disappears once the egg is beaten in.

Very refreshing when 'peckish' on a hot day.

Egg Flip

Serves 1

INGREDIENTS

1 egg
1 level teaspoon sugar (or to
  taste)

2 teaspoons sherry or brandy
¾ mug of milk

METHOD

1   Beat together the egg, sugar and sherry or brandy until
    smooth.
2   Heat the milk in a saucepan, but do not allow to boil.
3   Stir briskly into the mixture and serve at once in a
    tumbler or mug.

Peptail

Try this for breakfast or elevenses – it is a particularly nourishing beginning to the day if you do not fancy a cooked breakfast.

Serves 1

INGREDIENTS

1 egg	*or*, a small glass of carton or
the juice of 1 large orange	canned orange juice

Serve as cold as possible.

METHOD

1   In a jug, whisk the egg and orange juice together.
2   Strain out the small thread of the egg white by pouring through a strainer into a glass.

Notes: There is no flavour of raw egg in this refreshing pick-me-up.

The juice of the fresh orange was preferred by the cookery classes, but the others might make easier alternatives.

Lemonade

This makes a whole pint of lemonade from just one lemon. By keeping it in a covered glass jug you help to preserve the vitamin C overnight. You may have heard – correctly – that vitamin C is destroyed by storage. This is especially true of vegetables. But the acid of the lemon juice helps to preserve it from one day to the next.

INGREDIENTS

1 lemon   ½ pint of cold water
1½ rounded tablespoons
   caster sugar

METHOD

1 Wash the lemon and thinly peel just the outer yellow part of the rind.
2 Put the rind in a glass jug.
3 Squeeze the lemon and add the juice to the rind in the jug.
4 Stir in the sugar and water.
5 Leave it overnight, covered, in a cold, dark larder or – better still – in the refrigerator.
6 Next day, stir it again and make up to about a pint with cold water but taste it as you go along because you want it to have a tangy refreshing flavour.

For LIQUIDIZER LEMONADE, see page 242.

Chapter 3
Simple Recipes for One or Two

Contents

When planning meals:

You may often feel like cooking only one dish; it may be easier to buy a ready-prepared first course or to have fruit or something else uncooked for dessert. However, for those of you who wish to make fuller use of your oven, I have suggested ten two-course menus in which both first and second courses are cooked at the same oven temperature.

For even greater fuel economy, biscuits and cakes can be put in the oven to cook at the same temperature as the menu recipes. Suggestions are given in brackets.

Menu No. 1
Chicken Fiesta
Plum Betty
(Button Biscuits)

Menu No. 2
Scotch Eggs
Apple and Date
   Wholemeal Crumble
(Iced Buns)

Menu No. 3
Pork and Apple Slices
Potato Scones with
   Syrup

Menu No. 4
Seafood Square
Spiced Grapefruit
(Wholemeal Fruit
   Tartlets)

Menu No. 5
Liver and Bacon Bake
Baked Apple with Amber
   Sauce

Menu No. 6
Sausage Casserole
Orange Marmalade
   Sandwich Pudding

Menu No. 7
Meat Loaf with
   Jacket Potatoes
Apple Parcel
(Date and Lemon
   Flapjacks)

Menu No. 8
Roast Chicken
Shortcake Sandwich
(Date and Cherry Loaf)

Menu No. 9
Vegetable Layer
Bread Pudding

Menu No. 10
Savoury Soufflé
Prune Betty
(Muesli Biscuits)

Every recipe in the book is clearly marked with oven temperatures and time of cooking so that you can make up more menus of your own.

The chapters also include many top-of-the-stove recipes for both first course and dessert.

Mushroom Soup

Serves 2
Cooking time: approximately 15 minutes

INGREDIENTS

4 oz. washed and finely
   chopped mushrooms*
¼ pint of water
¼ chicken stock cube
½ pint of milk

1 oz. soft margarine
1 oz. plain flour, sieved
a pinch of mixed herbs
seasoning to taste
a little chopped parsley
   (optional)

* Chopping them takes only a few seconds with a food processor or a vegetable chopper (see page 266).

METHOD

1 Cook the chopped mushrooms gently in the water with a quarter stock cube for 5–10 minutes.
2 Remove from heat, add the milk first and then all other ingredients, apart from seasoning and parsley.
3 Return the pan to the heat and, whisking continuously with a flat or balloon whisk, bring to the boil and cook for 2–3 minutes.
4 Season to taste, and serve, sprinkled with a little chopped parsley.

Note: Although there are packets and cans of mushroom soup in the shops, the flavour of this home-made mushroom soup is so outstandingly good that we felt it worth inclusion in this book.

Carrot and Orange Soup

Serves 2 – hot or cold
Cooking time: about 40 minutes
You may like to make a second batch for the freezer: to get the
full benefit of vitamin C from the orange, freeze after Step 4.

INGREDIENTS

4 large carrots, peeled and
    sliced
small clove garlic, finely
    chopped
1 oz. butter or margarine
1 vegetable stock cube,
    made up with about ¾
    pint of water

1 level teaspoon white sugar
salt and pepper
grated rind and juice of ½ a
    small orange
1 oz. single cream, or top of
    the milk

METHOD

1   Using a heavy-based pan, fry the carrots and garlic
    gently in the melted fat for about 10 minutes, stirring
    occasionally.
2   Dissolve the stock cube in the boiling water and stir
    into the pan with the vegetables.
3   Bring to the boil, then reduce the heat and simmer, lid
    on, for 20–30 minutes until the carrots are cooked.
4   Remove from the heat and purée the soup through a
    Mouli or other sieve, or in a blender or food processor.
    Thin with more stock if necessary.
5   Return to heat, add sugar and adjust seasoning.
6   Just before serving stir in the grated rind and orange
    juice. Once the soup has been poured into the bowls,
    add a swirl of cream to each bowl.

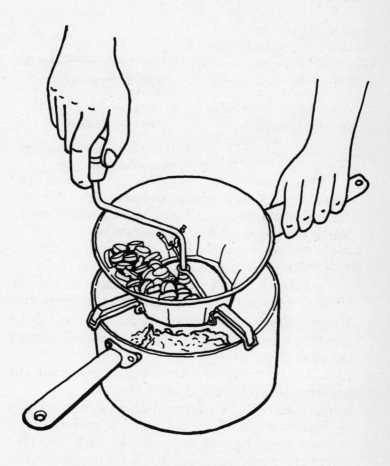

Egg and Lemon Sauce

INGREDIENTS

1 egg, size 1 or 2
juice of 1 lemon
¼ pint of chicken stock
(preferably use some of the
broth from Steamed
Roasting Chicken, page 98)

1 teaspoon granulated sugar,
or to taste
seasoning
parsley, cut roughly with
scissors (optional)

METHOD

1   Whisk the egg well in a small basin which you will
later be able to fit into the top of a small saucepan.
2   Stir in the lemon juice and the hot stock.
3   Place the basin over the saucepan which should contain an inch or two of near-boiling water. Keep the
water in the pan very gently simmering. Stir the contents of the basin until the sauce thickens enough to
coat the back of a wooden spoon.

4   Add sugar and seasoning to taste (this should be a sharp lemony sauce, so do not add too much sugar).
5   Stir in parsley and pour over the chicken, or serve in a separate sauce-boat.

Note: This is just as good cold with cold chicken – it thickens a little on cooling.

Tomato Sauce

INGREDIENTS

3 medium tomatoes, peeled*
  or 1 small can tomatoes
1 medium cooking apple

1–2 teaspoons vinegar
brown sugar

* To peel tomatoes, dip them into a pan of boiling water for less than a minute, put under cold water to make them easy to handle; the skin slips off easily.

Serve hot with fish or meat.

METHOD

1   Cut up peeled tomatoes, or use a small can of tomatoes, with peeled, cored, quartered cooking apple. Stew together till soft.
2   Add 1–2 teaspoons vinegar and sweeten to taste with brown sugar.

Eat within one or two days, reheating before use.

Curry Sauce

An economical way of 'stretching' cooked meat, fish, vegetables or eggs to make a substantial meal. Serves 2–3, can be reheated next day, so make it for 2 meals if you are living on your own.

Cooking time: 30–45 minutes

INGREDIENTS

a small knob of margarine
1 small onion, chopped
1 small sharp eating apple, peeled and finely chopped
1 to 2 level teaspoons curry powder
1 rounded tablespoon plain flour

½ pint of stock
1 teaspoon chutney
1 level teaspoon jam or marmalade
a few sultanas
salt and pepper
1 teaspoon vinegar or lemon juice

Serve with hard-boiled eggs, or with diced cooked meat, chicken, fish or vegetables. (Put into the curry sauce, bring to the boil, and simmer till hot – allow at least 15 minutes for cooked meat.)

METHOD

1   In a saucepan, melt the margarine and fry the onion, apple and curry powder together for 2–3 minutes.
2   Add all the remaining ingredients except the vinegar or lemon juice and, stirring continuously with a wooden spoon, bring to the boil. Cover and simmer gently for 30–45 minutes.
3   Add vinegar or lemon juice just before serving.

White Sauce *(all-in-one method)*

INGREDIENTS

Coating sauce
1 oz. butter or margarine
1 oz. flour
½ pint of milk
seasoning

Pouring sauce
¾ oz. butter or margarine
¾ oz. flour
½ pint of milk
seasoning

METHOD

1   Put all the ingredients into a small saucepan.
2   Heat slowly, stirring or whisking continually, until it comes to the boil.
3   Lower the heat and simmer gently, stirring all the time, for 3–5 minutes. Taste for seasoning.

Variations for White Sauce

After the sauce has boiled, you can stir in:
For cheese sauce – 2 heaped tablespoons grated cheese, a quarter teaspoon made mustard and a shake of cayenne pepper.
For egg sauce – 1 chopped hard-boiled egg.
For parsley sauce – 1 level tablespoon parsley, either chopped finely or snipped with scissors.

Low-Fat White Sauce

INGREDIENTS

Coating sauce
½ oz. cornflour
½ pint of skimmed or
  semi-skimmed milk
seasoning

Pouring sauce
¼ oz. cornflour
½ pint of skimmed or
  semi-skimmed milk
seasoning

METHOD

1 In a bowl blend the cornflour to a smooth paste with a little of the milk.
2 In a saucepan, heat the rest of the milk to boiling point.
3 Gradually stir the milk into the cornflour mixture.
4 Pour back into the saucepan and heat gently, stirring continuously, until thickened. Taste for seasoning.

Aubergine (or Courgette) and Tomatoes

Serves 2
Cooking time: 20 minutes

INGREDIENTS

1 slice bread (wholemeal or
   white)
1 small aubergine peeled and
   sliced
or 3 courgettes, peeled and
   sliced

2 large tomatoes, peeled*
   and halved
1 oz. butter or margarine
a sprinkling of sugar, salt
   and pepper
dash of Worcestershire sauce

(* for a reminder of the method, see page 55)

METHOD

1   Discard the crusts. Cut the bread into tiny cubes and put to one side.
2   Fry the prepared vegetables in the butter or margarine for about 15 minutes.
3   Season lightly with the sugar, salt, pepper and Worcestershire sauce.
4   Stir in the bread cubes and continue to fry to absorb some of the buttery juices.

Carrots and Leeks

Serves 2
Cooking time: approximately 20–30 minutes, according to size

INGREDIENTS

2 large carrots or 4 smaller
   carrots, peeled or scraped
2 leeks
1 oz. margarine or butter
1 oz. plain flour, sieved

¼ pint of milk
¼ pint of vegetable water
   drained from the cooked
   carrots and leeks
seasoning

METHOD

1   Wash the prepared carrots. Leeks are sometimes gritty and muddy. The easiest way to prepare them is to cut off the roots, then cut the leeks lengthwise in half. Wash them under running cold water, freeing the mud with your fingers as gently as possible to keep the leeks from falling apart. Give a final soak in cold water to make sure they are really free from grit.

2   Slice the carrots and leeks fairly thickly.

3   Boil together in lightly salted water till tender.

4   Drain off the cooking water into a bowl.

5   Into the pan with the drained carrots and leeks put the margarine, and when that has melted add the flour and half a pint of milk and vegetable water mixed.

6   Bring to the boil, stirring continuously, over low to medium heat. Allow the sauce to boil gently for about 3 minutes.

7   Adjust seasoning to taste before serving.

Note: Other vegetables can be cooked together in one pan, drained and then mashed together with a little margarine or butter and seasoning; you may find this simpler than making the sauce as above. Try a mixture of *potato and parsnip* or *potato and swede*.

Carrots (or Parsnips) Cooked in Butter

This is not only one of the tastiest ways of cooking carrots or parsnips but also the most sensible – unless of course you are on a low-fat diet. Root vegetables easily absorb fat. By cooking not in water but in butter, you help to conserve nourishment.

Cooking time: sliced old carrots or parsnips – 10–20 minutes
whole new carrots – up to 45 minutes

You need a thick saucepan with a really tight-fitting lid. (This is essential because the vegetables cook in the steam from their own moisture, and they produce so little steam that none of it must escape.)

If the lid of your saucepan does not fit tightly, use instead an enamel plate with weights on top to keep it down or an improvised lid of kitchen foil.

INGREDIENTS

carrots or parsnips
a large knob of butter
seasoning

a pinch of sugar
chopped parsley (optional)

METHOD

1   Scrub and scrape or peel the carrots and cut older carrots into even slices, not too thick. New carrots can be left whole. Parsnips need to be peeled and sliced.
2   Heat sufficient butter to cover well the bottom of the pan. When it is hot but not smoking, add the carrots or parsnips.
3   Add salt and pepper, but not too much because none of its flavour will be lost.
4   Cover with lid and cook over a *gentle* heat, shaking the pan occasionally so that the vegetables do not stick or burn. Sliced carrots or parsnips will take 10–20 minutes to become tender according to thickness. Whole new carrots may take up to 45 minutes.
5   Sprinkle with a good pinch of granulated or caster sugar – this helps to bring out the natural flavour of the vegetable. Also sprinkle with coarsely chopped parsley if you like the extra colour and flavour.
6   Serve with any buttery juices still remaining.

Cauliflower Savoury

Serves 2

INGREDIENTS

a 4-oz. can condensed
   mushroom soup
4 tablespoons milk
1 small cauliflower, divided
   into sprigs and cooked

2 eggs, hard-boiled and
   chopped
1 thin slice lightly buttered
   bread
tomatoes or watercress

Serve with tomatoes or watercress.

METHOD

1   Place the soup and milk in a small saucepan and heat
    gently to make a thick sauce.
2   Place the sprigs of cooked cauliflower in an oven-proof
    dish.
3   Add the chopped eggs.
4   Pour the mushroom sauce over the cauliflower
    mixture.
5   Cut the bread into small squares and place on top,
    butter side up. Grill till golden brown.

Note: For one serving, cook approximately 4 oz. fresh or
frozen cauliflower florets and hard boil 1 egg. Make up the
same quantity of mushroom sauce.

Potatoes Baked in their Jackets

Oven temperature: 400°F, 200°C, gas mark 6
Cooking time: 45 minutes–1 hour

INGREDIENTS

even-sized, unblemished   a little butter or margarine
   potatoes

METHOD

1   Choose one medium-sized (4–6 oz.) potato per person.
2   Scrub well and dry (or buy pre-washed potatoes and
    merely rinse and dry, if necessary).
3   Prick all over, through the skin, with a fork.
4   Rub the skin with butter or margarine, using grease-
    proof paper or the wrapping paper from the fat to avoid
    messy handling. This makes the skin delicious to eat.
5   Place on a baking tray or direct on the oven shelf, and
    bake at 400°F, 200°C, gas mark 6 for 45 minutes to 1
    hour, according to size. When ready, they feel soft if
    squeezed gently with a cloth.
6   Cut lengthwise in halves and mash in plenty of butter.

Notes: For even cooking right through to the centre,
impale the raw potato on a skewer or metal potato baker.
   To make a snack meal, mash in a choice of filling, e.g.:
      – sour cream, cottage or cream cheese
      – grated cheese and pickle
      – hot baked beans and sausage
      – tuna and sweetcorn

Potato Gratin

A variation on a popular French dish, one of the recipes sent to me by a friend, Madeleine Carnazzi.

Serves 1
Oven temperature: 350°F, 180°C, gas mark 4
Cooking time: about 45 minutes

INGREDIENTS

1 potato (6–8 oz.), peeled
salt, pepper, pinch of
   nutmeg

1 oz. Gruyère cheese
1 egg yolk
¼ pint of milk

· This can be served with grilled bacon, garnished with watercress.

METHOD

1 Cut the potato into thin slices.
2 Place a layer of potato in a small, buttered pie dish or shallow casserole. Season lightly. Top with half the cheese, grated or sliced wafer thin.
3 Repeat layers of potato, seasoning and cheese.
4 Beat the egg yolk into the milk, season and pour over the potato and cheese.
5 Bake, uncovered, at 350°F, 180°C, gas mark 4 for about 45 minutes, until the potato is soft and the custard set and golden.

Note: Use the extra egg white in fruit purées.

Vegetables, Chinese Style

This recipe can be prepared in a wok, an electric frying pan or an ordinary frying pan covered with a lid or foil.

Serves 1–2
Cooking time: 5–6 minutes

INGREDIENTS

2 slender carrots
quarter of a small green
  pepper
1 small onion, peeled

3–4 mushrooms
1 tablespoon salad oil
1 tablespoon hot water
salt and pepper

METHOD

1 Wash and scrape or peel the carrots. Slice into thin coins or diagonal slices.
2 Cut the green pepper into thin slices, and slice the onion and mushrooms thinly.
3 Heat the oil in small frying pan or wok over moderate heat for about 2 minutes.
4 Reduce the heat to low, add the vegetables, and stir constantly for 1 minute.
5 Add the hot water, season lightly, stir the mixture, and cover the pan tightly. Let the vegetables steam in the moisture over low heat for 3–4 minutes, or until they are tender but still crisp. Serve immediately.

Vegetable Layer

Serves 2
Oven temperature: 350°F, 180°C, gas mark 4
Cooking time: approx. 1 hour 15 minutes

INGREDIENTS

8 oz. potatoes, peeled and
   thinly sliced
3 oz. streaky bacon, chopped
4 oz. carrots, peeled and
   sliced

2 oz. frozen sliced green
   beans
2 oz. Cheddar cheese, grated
1 egg
¼ pint of milk
salt and pepper

METHOD

1   Grease a one-and-a-quarter-pint ovenproof pie dish.
2   Layer half of the potato, bacon, carrots, beans and
    grated cheese into the dish.
3   Repeat, using up all these ingredients and finish with a
    layer of cheese.
4   Beat together egg, milk and a light sprinkling of salt
    and pepper. Pour over the ingredients in the dish.
5   Bake at 350°F, 180°C, gas mark 4 until cooked right
    through, set and golden.

Vegetables, Steamed

This delicious method of cooking vegetables is thoroughly recommended by a reader, Miss Mary Lister. She enjoys vegetables so much that she often has as many as five different kinds at one meal, using two steamer baskets. Their delightful mixed flavours go well with any meat, chicken or fish.

Cooking time: according to the varieties steamed, it can take from 5–30 minutes

INGREDIENTS

Any suitable mixture of vegetables, e.g., potatoes, carrots, broccoli or cauliflower sprigs, runner beans, leeks, celery, brussels sprouts . . .

METHOD

1   Prepare the vegetables and – according to variety – slice fairly thinly, or divide into small sprigs. Potatoes, well scrubbed, can be left in their skins and cut small.
2   Place in a steamer basket or metal colander, sprinkle with a little salt or with a generous squeeze of lemon juice and a good pinch of herbs. Potatoes and carrots, which need the longest cooking (up to 30 minutes) should be put in the steamer basket first. The other vegetables can be added later.
3   To steam, place the steamer basket into a saucepan and pour round it enough boiling water to come to the top of the tiny legs of the basket. There should be no water touching the vegetables inside the steamer.

4   Place over a high heat and as soon as the water returns
    to the boil – this takes only seconds – reduce the heat
    to keep it simmering gently with the lid tightly on.
5   After 15 minutes put in the other sliced vegetables,
    adding courgettes during the last 5 minutes of cooking
    time.

Note: You will need a small steamer basket. One inexpensive type is made of stainless steel; it opens up like a
flower to be filled and closes down again for storage.

Alternative: Use a metal colander balanced in the
saucepan so that it fits well down without touching the
water; the steam will come up through the holes and will
be prevented from leaving by the lid over the vegetables.

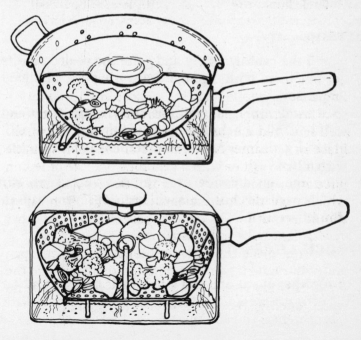

Coleslaw 'Make-ahead'

This is a coleslaw to have on hand when you are unable to prepare a last-minute salad. It also makes a welcome home-made gift when visiting. The acid of the vinegar dressing helps to retain vitamin C.

Serves 4

INGREDIENTS

quarter of a medium-sized white cabbage
4 medium-sized carrots
3–4 tablespoons vinegar
3 tablespoons sugar
2 tablespoons salad oil
salt, pepper
garlic powder (optional)

METHOD

1   Shred the cabbage finely and grate the peeled carrots (or put them both through the grating disc of a food processor).
2   In a small saucepan combine the vinegar, sugar and salad oil, plus a light seasoning of salt and pepper and, if liked, garlic powder. Bring to the boil and simmer for 3 minutes.
3   Pour the hot dressing over the raw vegetables, stir well, cover and chill. This will keep for several days in the refrigerator.

French Dressing

Fork together about one and a half tablespoons salad oil with half a tablespoon of vinegar, seasoning to taste with salt, pepper, mustard and sugar.

Tomato and Orange Salad

Serves 2

INGREDIENTS

2 medium tomatoes
1 orange
1 large teaspoon chopped
  parsley

a few finely chopped spring
  onions *or* chives
2 tablespoons French
  dressing

METHOD

1 Slice the tomatoes.
2 Cut the skin from orange with a sharp knife and cut
    out the juicy segments.*
3 Arrange the slices of tomato alternately with the
    orange.
4 Sprinkle with chopped parsley, spring onions or chives
    and moisten with French dressing.

* If you find it easier, just cut the peeled orange across in slices
and then into wedges.

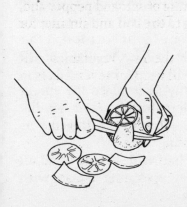
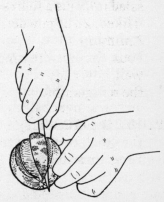

Cheese and Cress Omelette

Serves 1

INGREDIENTS

2 eggs
1 tablespoon water
salt and pepper
½ oz. butter
1½ oz. Cheddar cheese
(sliced, then broken in
pieces)

2–3 sprigs of watercress
(roughly cut up with
scissors) or some mustard
and cress* (cut with
scissors)

* Nowadays this is generally bought as 'growing cress' so that
a little can be cut off at a time, and the rest will keep fresh.

METHOD

1   Beat the eggs, water and seasoning together in a small
bowl.
2   Heat the butter in an omelette pan, or small frying-
pan, and pour the egg mixture into it.
3   Cook quickly, drawing the outside cooked mixture
towards centre with a fork. Then tilt the pan so the
uncooked mixture goes to the edge (it is easiest at this
stage to use a palette knife to lift the edges of the
omelette).
4   Cook until the top is creamy, then place the cheese
and cress over half the omelette furthest from handle.
5   Fold the other half of the omelette over filling and tip
the omelette out on to a serving plate.
6   Serve immediately.

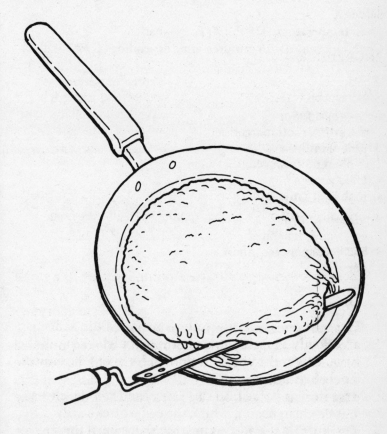

Cheese Soufflé, One-stage

Serves 2
Oven temperature: 375°F, 190°C, gas mark 5
Cooking time: 20–25 minutes (time depending on size of dish)

INGREDIENTS

One-stage sauce
1 oz. butter or soft margarine
¼ pint of milk
1 oz. plain flour, sieved
salt and pepper
a pinch of dry mustard

To finish soufflé
2 eggs, size 4, separated
3 oz. Cheddar cheese, finely
   grated

METHOD

1   Place all the sauce ingredients in a medium saucepan
    and slowly bring to the boil, stirring or whisking all the
    time. Lower the heat and simmer for about 3 minutes.
    Cool slightly.
2   Beat the egg yolks into this sauce, and add the cheese.
3   With a clean beater, whisk the egg whites stiffly.
4   Cut and fold the whites into the sauce until the soufflé
    is evenly mixed (it is easiest to do this with a metal
    tablespoon).
5   Pour into a greased one-and-a-half to two-pint oven-
    proof dish which will allow room for the mixture to

rise (preferably a soufflé case with straight sides) and bake on the middle shelf of a pre-heated oven, 375°F, 190°C, gas mark 5, for 20–25 minutes, according to the size of the dish. Serve immediately.

Potato Omelette

This is a tasty way of using up small amounts of left-over cooked vegetables from the refrigerator.

Serves 1

INGREDIENTS

a knob of butter or
   margarine
1 medium-sized boiled
   potato, cubed
1 small raw onion, chopped
2 tablespoons cooked
   vegetables, such as peas,
   beans, carrots or
   sweetcorn
2 eggs
1 tablespoon water
salt and pepper

METHOD

1   In an omelette pan or small frying pan, heat the butter or margarine until it begins to turn colour. Add the potato and onion and cook, stirring, until lightly browned.
2   Stir in the other vegetables.
3   With a fork, lightly beat together the eggs and water, adding a little pepper and salt.
4   Be sure the vegetables are loosened from the pan, and add a little more butter if necessary. Pour the egg mixture over, then twirl the pan to distribute well up the sides.
5   When the edges look dry, loosen with a knife, allowing any uncooked egg to flow underneath. When just cooked, fold in half. Turn on to a hot plate and serve immediately.

Savoury Sandwich Puddings

Don't waste left-over sandwiches: turn them into a pudding. Or use fresh sandwiches . . .

Cheese and Tomato Sandwich Pudding

Serves 1–2
Oven temperature: 350°F, 180°C, gas mark 4
Cooking time: 30 minutes

INGREDIENTS

2 slices wholemeal or brown
   bread
butter or margarine
Marmite
thinly sliced cheese

1 small tomato, sliced
1 egg
just under ¼ pint of milk (6
   tablespoons)
seasoning

METHOD

1 Make a savoury sandwich, e.g. spread bread thinly with butter and Marmite, and fill with slices of cheese and tomato. After removing crusts, cut into squares or strips and arrange in small oven-proof dish.
2 Beat up the egg and milk, adding a shake of pepper and a pinch of mustard.
3 Pour over the sandwiches and bake for about 30 minutes until set, at 350°F, 180°C, gas mark 4.

Other suggested sandwich fillings: cheese and pickle, ham and tomato.

Welsh Rarebit

Serves 1
Cooking time: approximately 5 minutes

INGREDIENTS

a knob of soft margarine
2 oz. Cheddar cheese, grated
2 teaspoons milk
3–4 drops Worcestershire
  sauce

a pinch of dry mustard
1 large slice, or 2 small slices,
  of bread, toasted and
  spread with margarine

METHOD

1   Mix all the ingredients together with a wooden spoon.
2   Spread over the toast.
3   Place under a hot grill until golden and serve
    immediately.

Welsh Rarebit de Luxe

1. *Buck Rarebit*
A poached egg placed on the grilled Welsh Rarebit.

2. *Bacon*
A grilled rasher or two placed on the grilled Welsh Rarebit.

3. *Tomato*
A sliced tomato placed on the toast, covered with the Welsh Rarebit and then grilled.

4. *Chicken or Ham*
Slices or pieces of cooked chicken or cooked ham placed on the toast, covered with the Welsh Rarebit and then grilled.

5. *Apple*
Thin slices of peeled crisp eating apple placed on the toast, covered with the Welsh Rarebit and then grilled.

Cod Charlotte

Comment from Harlow Technical College: 'No difficulty at all, and all liked the crispy cubes of bread on top of the fish. We served frozen peas with this, with the Lemon Sponge Pudding (see page 190) to follow.'

Serves 2
Oven temperature: 350°F, 180°C, gas mark 4
Cooking time: 35–40 minutes

INGREDIENTS

2 cod steaks
2 eggs
¼ pint of milk
1 tablespoon chopped
    parsley (it is easiest to snip
    the parsley roughly with
    kitchen scissors)

salt and pepper
3 slices of bread about half
    an inch thick, crusts
    removed
about 1½ oz. margarine

METHOD

1   Place the cod steaks in a greased ovenproof dish.
2   Beat together the eggs and milk and add parsley and seasoning. Pour over the fish.
3   Cut the slices of bread into half-inch cubes.
4   Melt the margarine in a pan, add the bread cubes, and toss until coated.
5   Cover the fish with the bread cubes, and bake in a moderate oven 350°F, 180°C, gas mark 4 for 35–40 minutes.

Grilled Cod

Serves 1 or 2
Cooking time: approximately 15 minutes

INGREDIENTS

2 cod cutlets (or 1 cutlet per
   person) and a little
   margarine
1 oz. Cheddar cheese

1 oz. margarine
seasoning
a little milk

METHOD

1 Place the cod cutlet, dotted with a little margarine, on
   the greased grill pan, and cook under a medium grill for
   about 5 or 6 minutes, according to the thickness of the
   cutlet.
2 Grate or crumble the cheese and mix with the 1 oz.
   margarine, the seasoning and a little milk, until it is of
   spreading consistency.
3 Remove cutlet from under grill. Turn the fish over and
   spread with the cheese mixture.
4 Grill gently for a further 6–10 minutes.

Fish Soufflé

Serves 2
Oven temperature: 350–375°F, 180–190°C, gas mark 4–5
Cooking time: 20–30 minutes

INGREDIENTS

8 oz. cooked white fish*   salt and pepper
2 eggs   tomato ketchup
                                             mixed herbs

Serve with extra tomato ketchup, or QUICK TOMATO
SAUCE, page 17.

* *To steam the fish:* Place on an enamel or other heatproof
plate, dot with butter or margarine, moisten with a little milk,
season with pepper and salt. Cover with an upturned plate, or
the lid of the saucepan. Place the plate of fish on top of the
saucepan, in which there are a few inches of gently simmering
water – keep simmering on top of the stove. Make sure the
plate is large enough to balance easily on top of the saucepan,
and lift it off with oven gloves when the fish is cooked (when it
is opaque and soft) to prevent scalding yourself in the steam
from the pan.

Alternatively, as you will be using the oven later, you may
prefer baking for the preliminary cooking of the fish.

To bake the fish: Place in a baking tin with the butter or
margarine, milk and seasoning, cover and bake for 20 minutes
– or longer for a thick cut – at 375°F, 190°C, gas mark 5.

METHOD

1   Separate eggs and beat the yolks into the hot flaked
     fish. Season with pepper and salt and flavour well with
     tomato ketchup and a good pinch of mixed herbs.

2   Whisk egg whites stiffly and fold into the fish mixture.
3   Pile into a buttered ovenproof dish, leaving room for soufflé to rise, and bake in a pre-heated oven 350°–375°F, 180–190°C, gas mark 4–5, for 20–30 minutes, depending on the size of dish and the temperature used.

Grilled Marinated Fish

Serves 2
Cooking time: approximately 12–15 minutes

INGREDIENTS

2 fish steaks (fresh cod or salmon)
a small knob of butter
4 tablespoons sunflower oil

4 teaspoons lemon juice
pinch of dried mixed herbs
2 trimmed spring onions

METHOD

1   Generously butter a small flameproof shallow casserole.
2   Beat together the oil, lemon juice and herbs and pour into the casserole dish. Add the snipped or sliced spring onions.
3   Place fish in this marinade and leave for a couple of hours, basting occasionally.
4   Grill in the dish under moderate heat till cooked through, turning once (approximately 6–8 minutes on each side, depending on thickness).

One-pot Kedgeree

This is a useful recipe if you have only one cooking ring, or if you want to save fuel and washing up by using only one pot. The method may sound complicated, but try it; it is very easy.

Serves 2–3 (can be served hot one day, cold the next)
 Or, for 1 person, halve quantities but cook all the haddock and use half for SCRAMBLED HADDOCK AND EGGS (see page 30) next day.
Cooking time: about 20 minutes

INGREDIENTS

a 7½-oz. packet
  Boil-in-the-Bag Buttered
  Smoked Haddock
2 oz. long-grain rice
2 eggs, rinsed under the tap
  just before use

3–4 tablespoons salad cream
1 tablespoon chopped
  parsley
salt and pepper
lettuce leaves and tomato
  wedges (when served cold)

METHOD

1 Bring about 3 pints of water to the boil in a large pan, and place the boil-in-the-bag fish, the rice, and eggs (left in their shells) in the pan.
2 Return to the boil and simmer for 12 minutes.
3 Remove the eggs and run them under cold water. Simmer the fish and rice for a further 5 minutes.
4 Remove the bag of fish and allow to cool.
  Strain the rice.

5 Shell and chop or slice the eggs.
Remove the fish from the bag, but do not throw away the liquor.
Skin and flake the fish.
Mix eggs and fish with the rice.
Add the liquor from the bag.
6 Add the salad cream and parsley and season to taste.

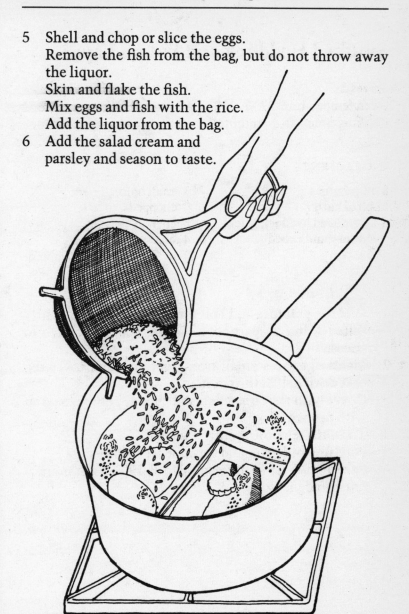

Smoked Haddock and Potato Layer

Serves 2
Oven temperature: 375°F, 190°C, gas mark 5
Cooking time: 20–25 minutes

INGREDIENTS

8 oz. potatoes
knob of butter
8 oz. smoked haddock fillet,
    skinned and cubed

1 small onion, finely
    chopped
pepper
4 tablespoons milk
2 oz. Cheddar cheese, grated

METHOD

1   Peel the potatoes and boil for 5–10 minutes in lightly
    salted water to part-cook. Drain, cool and cut into
    slices.
2   Lightly grease a small ovenproof dish and cover the
    base with half of the potato.
3   Cover with the cubed fish and chopped onion. Season
    with pepper.
4   Top with remaining potato slices.
5   Pour the milk over and sprinkle with cheese.
6   Bake for 20–25 minutes at 375°F, 190°C, gas mark 5
    until golden.

Seafish Crumble

Serves 1
Oven temperature: 350°F, 180°C, gas mark 4
Cooking time: about 20 minutes

INGREDIENTS

Fish sauce
1 oz. butter
1 oz. flour
¼ pint of milk
pinch of mustard
salt and pepper

6 oz. cod or coley fillet
  or smoked cod or
  haddock, skinned and
  cubed
2 oz. frozen peas

Crumble topping
½ oz. butter
1 oz. wholemeal flour
1 oz. Cheddar cheese, grated

METHOD

1   For the fish sauce, place the butter, flour and milk in a saucepan and heat gently, stirring until thickened.
2   Season with mustard and salt and pepper, and continue cooking and stirring for 1 minute.
3   Remove from the heat and stir in the fish and peas. Pour into an ovenproof dish.
4   To make the crumble, rub butter into flour and stir in the cheese. Spoon over the fish mixture.
5   Bake in the oven at 350°F, 180°C, gas mark 4 for 15–20 minutes until the topping is bubbling and golden.

Summer Fish

Serves 1

INGREDIENTS

1 small can mackerel fillets
   in brine *or* tuna fish *or*
   salmon
half a lemon

1 teaspoon chopped mint
1 teaspoon chopped parsley
seasoning
salad cream

This looks attractive served on a bed of shredded lettuce.

METHOD

1   Drain the fish – the bones of salmon can be mashed
    into the fish.
2   Mix the fish with the juice of half a lemon and the
    chopped mint and parsley.
3   Season to taste with salt and pepper.
4   Decorate with a little salad cream.

Note: This can also be used as a sandwich filling.

Sausage Pilau

This is a simple and economical way to make sausages more tempting and the whole dish is cooked together in one pan.

Serves 1
Cooking time: about 25 minutes

INGREDIENTS

1 tablespoon oil
2 sausages, cut into chunks
2 tablespoons raw rice
half a small onion, chopped
or 3 spring onions, snipped
1 oz. mushrooms, sliced

1 teaspoon Worcestershire
  sauce
salt and pepper
¼ pint of water or stock
2 oz. frozen mixed
  vegetables

METHOD

1   Using a small saucepan, brown the sausages in the oil – this will take about 7 minutes.
2   Add the rice, onion and mushrooms and cook again for 2–3 minutes.
3   Stir in the Worcestershire sauce, a little seasoning, and the liquid.
4   Cover and simmer for 15 minutes or until the rice has absorbed most of the liquid. Meanwhile, add the vegetables to the pan, to cook according to the instructions on the packet.
5   Adjust the seasoning and serve immediately.

Liver and Bacon Bake

Serves 2 (or halve quantities for one serving)
Oven temperature: 350°F, 180°C, gas mark 4
Cooking time: 45 minutes

INGREDIENTS

2 slices of lamb's or pig's
    liver
stock made with a little
    Marmite or Bovril

2 tablespoons packet
    stuffing mix
4 rashers streaky bacon

METHOD

1   Put the liver in an ovenproof dish.
2   Barely cover with the Marmite or Bovril stock.
3   Make up the 2 tablespoons of stuffing with boiling
    water as directed on the packet.
4   Spread the stuffing on top of the liver.
5   Top with the bacon rashers.
6   Bake uncovered in a moderate oven at 350°F, 180°C,
    gas mark 4 for 45 minutes.

Devilled Kidneys

Serves 1
Cooking time: 10 minutes

INGREDIENTS

2 lamb's kidneys
a knob of butter
1 rasher of bacon
1 slice of toast
tomato or other vegetable

1 teaspoon vinegar
1 small flat teaspoon of
   made mustard
a sprinkling of pepper and
   salt

METHOD

1 Cut the kidneys in half and, with pointed scissors, remove the inner core and then peel off the skin.
2 Fry the halved kidneys gently in butter for 8 minutes, turning them once or twice.
3 Meanwhile, start grilling the bacon (and tomato, if you like it cooked) and making the toast.
4 Stir the vinegar, mustard, pepper and salt into the kidney pan. Cook 2 minutes more.
5 Serve on toast with bacon and tomato or other vegetable.

Bacon Joint, Glazed

Serves 4: enough for a hot meal for 2 on one day and a cold
meal for 2 on the second day
Oven temperature: 375°F, 190°C, gas mark 5, 10–15 minutes,
after preliminary 30 minutes simmer on top of stove (or follow
cooking instructions if using a pre-packed joint)

INGREDIENTS

1¼–1½-lb. bacon joint
1 teaspoon black treacle

1 tablespoon brown sugar
2 teaspoons made mustard
2 tablespoons sherry or
water

METHOD

1　Place the bacon in a pan of cold water. Bring to the boil
and simmer for 30 minutes. (Taste the water: if necessary throw off the water once it has boiled, to remove
excess salty flavour, and then bring to the boil again
with fresh water and simmer. This is not generally
necessary with small ready-to-cook packed joints.)
2　Remove the bacon from the water. Strip off any rind.
Mix treacle, sugar, mustard and sherry or water to a
smooth paste and spread over the fat on top of the
bacon joint.
3　Place in a small roasting tin in fairly hot oven
(375°F, 190°C, gas mark 5) for 10–15 minutes, *basting
frequently* to avoid drying out.

Bacon or Ham with Mustard Sauce

Serves 2
Oven temperature: 400°F, 200°C, gas mark 6
Cooking time: 25–30 minutes

Note: If you want to serve one, halve the amount of bacon or ham but keep to the full quantity of sauce.

INGREDIENTS

2 *thick-cut* lean rashers of bacon (long back or collar) or 2 ham steaks
1 tablespoon made mustard (or use 1 tablespoon dry mustard powder plus a little water)

1 level tablespoon soft brown sugar
2 level teaspoons plain flour
4 tablespoons milk

METHOD

1   Remove the bacon rind and place the rashers or the ham steaks in a casserole.
2   Mix the mustard, sugar and flour together and add the milk gradually, stirring well, until smooth. Pour over the rashers, and cover the casserole.
3   Bake in a preheated oven at 400°F, 200°C, gas mark 6 for 25–30 minutes.
4   Dish up the rashers on to a hot serving dish or plates, stir the sauce in the casserole and pour over the rashers.

Bacon Pudding

Although this recipe calls for mincing or grating three separate items, we felt it worth including because it is so economical.

Serves 2 or 3 – good served cold next day
Cooking time: 1½–2 hours

INGREDIENTS

½ oz. margarine, melted
½ pint (or one large cup) soft breadcrumbs
1 egg, beaten

½ level teaspoon mixed herbs
4 oz. bacon pieces ⎫ minced
1 small onion ⎭ together
2 oz. cheese, grated or crumbled

Serve hot with greens and potatoes and tomato sauce, or cold with salad.

METHOD

1 Mix all ingredients together (note – no seasoning is required because bacon is salty).
2 Pack into a small well-greased 1-pint basin.
3 Cover with kitchen foil or tie on a double thickness of greaseproof paper.
4 Steam, or stand the bowl in a pan of boiling water, topping up the water occasionally so that it stays about two thirds up the outside of the bowl. Steam with the lid tightly on the pan for 1½ to 2 hours.

Chicken Casserole

Serves 1
Cooking time: 40 minutes

INGREDIENTS

1 oz. margarine
1 chicken portion
1 small onion, sliced, or 1
    tablespoon dried onion
1 tomato, quartered
¼ pint stock (or ¼ cube of
    chicken stock dissolved in
    water)

1–2 oz. mushrooms, sliced
    (if you buy ¼ lb.
    mushrooms, use the rest
    for mushroom omelette or
    for mushrooms on toast)
2 teaspoons tomato purée
salt and pepper (optional)

METHOD

1   Take a saucepan with a lid, heat margarine and fry the
    chicken and onion (if using fresh) for 8–10 minutes.
    Pour off the fat. This can be used for other frying.
2   Add the remaining ingredients (if using dried onion,
    include at this stage).
3   Stir well, bring to the boil and simmer with the lid on
    for 30 minutes. Check flavour and add seasoning if
    necessary. You may find sufficient flavour has been
    provided by the stock cube.

Chicken Fiesta

Serves 2, plus an extra portion that could be used cold for sandwiches, made into a chicken salad or frozen for another meal.
Top of stove or oven cooking
Oven temperature: 375°F, 190°C, gas mark 5
Cooking time (either method): approximately 1 hour

INGREDIENTS

3 chicken portions
half a 15-oz. can tomato
  soup (*not* cream of
  tomato)*
half a 15-oz. can chicken
  consommé *or* oxtail soup*

1½ teaspoons dried thyme
4 tablespoons raw long-grain
  rice
green vegetables

*   The remaining half-cans of soup can be combined for a delicious, warming soup for next day. Patricia Coleman's original recipe in Canada used chicken consommé, but where this is not available oxtail soup makes a well-flavoured substitute.

METHOD (oven)

1   Place the chicken portions in a baking dish. Combine the undiluted soups and the thyme and pour over the chicken.
2   Cover the dish and bake at 375°F, 190°C, gas mark 5 for 1 hour, or until tender. Baste frequently during cooking.
3   Serve with boiled rice and green vegetables.

METHOD (top of stove)

1   Stir the two soups together in a saucepan. Add the
    chicken portions.
2   Sprinkle in the thyme and then the well washed rice.
3   Bring to the boil, then turn the heat down to simmer
    gently. Stir. Cover with the pan lid and simmer for
    50–60 minutes, stirring occasionally.
4   Serve with green vegetables.

Steamed Roasting Chicken

Cooking time: 1¼ hours approximately

INGREDIENTS

1 small whole roasting
    chicken*
1 small onion
1 small carrot

1 bay leaf
a thin strip of lemon rind
1 teaspoon salt
the chicken giblets

* If using a frozen chicken, de-frost it thoroughly.

Serve with EGG AND LEMON SAUCE (p. 54).

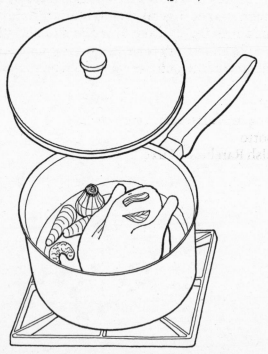

METHOD

1   Use a saucepan with a well-fitting lid just slightly larger than the washed and trussed chicken.
2   Pour into the saucepan about 1 inch of cold water, add the peeled onion and carrot, the bay leaf, lemon rind, salt and giblets. Lastly put in the chicken.
3   Bring to the boil, skim if necessary, put the lid on the pan and turn the heat down so that the water simmers gently. A small chicken weighing two and three quarter pounds or a little more will take about one hour 15 minutes.

This makes a very tender chicken for eating hot and the stock makes a good strong broth for chicken soup. Steamed roasting chicken is moist and succulent when eaten cold, far less dry than cold roasted chicken.

Other recipes which use cooked chicken include:
Pilaff
Curry
Chicken Fricassée in One Pan
Risotto
Welsh Rarebit de Luxe

Chicken Fricassée in One Pan

Serves 2
Cooking time: 8–10 minutes

INGREDIENTS

1 oz. margarine
1 small onion, peeled and
   chopped or sliced
2 oz. mushrooms, washed
   and sliced
1 oz. margarine
1 oz. plain flour
½ pint of milk

salt and pepper to taste
about 6 oz. cooked chicken,
   cut into small pieces
small can of peas, drained
a slice of bread, toasted and
   cut into fingers
wedges of lemon

METHOD

1   Melt 1 oz. margarine in saucepan and fry the onion and
    the mushrooms until softened but not browned.
2   To make the sauce, add the next ounce of margarine,
    with the flour, milk and seasoning, to the pan of
    onions and mushrooms. Whisking all the time with a
    balloon whisk, bring to the boil and cook for 2–3
    minutes. (It is possible to whisk vigorously with a fork,
    but it is less tiring and more efficient to use a balloon
    whisk. See illustration p. 170.)
3   Add the chicken and peas and reheat.
4   Pour into serving dish or on to plates and garnish with
    fingers of toast and wedges of lemon. (For a delicious
    flavour, squeeze the lemon into the fricassée before
    eating.)

Chops and Onions

Serves 1
Cooking time: approximately 15 minutes for thin cutlets,
anything up to about 35 minutes for a thick chop

INGREDIENTS

butter or margarine
1 small to medium onion,
    peeled and sliced
1 lamb chop or 2 small
    cutlets

1 tablespoon of flour, mixed
    with a little salt and
    pepper

Most people like lamb well done in the middle so that a
skewer or sharp knife pushed into the centre will not bring out
a fluid too red or pink.

METHOD

1   If using thin cutlets, start frying the sliced onion in the
    pan about 5 minutes *before* adding the meat. For thick
    chops, add the onion to the pan about 15 minutes *after*
    the meat.
2   To fry the chop or cutlets: wash and pat dry with
    kitchen paper, and dust with the seasoned flour.
        Fry in the butter with the onion, turning the meat
    over occasionally until it is cooked well through and
    beginning to crisp and brown.
3   Remove the chop or cutlets on to the plate and keep
    warm.
4   Very carefully pour into the pan of onions just a little
    water.
5   Stir it around, bring to the boil and you will have plump

onions in a lovely golden buttery liquor to pour over the chop.

Note: These plump buttery onions are also delicious poured over fried steak or liver or – far less expensive – beefburgers.

Easy Chilli

Serves 2
Cooking time: 25–30 minutes

INGREDIENTS

8 oz. lean minced beef   1 small can of kidney beans
half a small onion   1 medium can of tomatoes
a small stalk of celery, sliced ½–1 teaspoon chilli powder

Serve with rice and green salad (without dressing).

METHOD

1   Brown the meat in a frying pan. Drain off excess fat.
2   Add the onion and celery and heat, stirring, for 3–4
     minutes.
3   Add the drained kidney beans, chopped tomatoes
     (with their juice) and chilli powder.
4   Simmer over low heat for 20 minutes, or longer if a
     thicker mixture is desired.

Note: Because chilli is good made ahead and reheated,
you might want to double the recipe and have planned
left-overs.

Lancashire Hot-pot

Serves 2, or one serving one day, the rest cooled quickly then *thoroughly* reheated for a second serving next day. Cooked in the oven or on top of the stove depending on rest of meal.
Oven temperature: 350°F, 180°C, gas mark 4
Cooking time: 1 hour 30 minutes

INGREDIENTS

4 pieces neck of lamb
1 medium onion
1 carrot
2 medium potatoes
piece of celery, if available
piece of turnip (optional)

seasoning
1 teaspoon Bovril
¼ pint of water
a little chopped parsley
  (optional)

METHOD

1   Wash the meat.
2   Prepare vegetables and cut up small, except for one potato.
3   Place vegetables and meat in layers in casserole or saucepan and add seasoning.
4   Dissolve Bovril in the hot water and add to the meat and vegetables.
5   Slice the remaining potato thinly and arrange on top. Cover casserole or pan with lid.
6   *For cooking on top of the stove:*
    Bring pan to the boil, reduce heat to the lowest and simmer for 1 hour 30 minutes.

For cooking in the oven:
Place casserole in the oven at 350°F, 180°C, gas mark 4 for 45 minutes. Remove from oven, remove lid, and brush potatoes with melted fat, leave lid off and cook for at least a further 45 minutes.

Serve sprinkled with chopped parsley.

Meat Stew, Norwegian Style

Serves 2 – or one serving one day, the second serving next day.
Cooking time: 1 hour 30 minutes
You will need a medium-sized saucepan with a tightly fitting lid.

INGREDIENTS

8 oz. stewing steak
half a cabbage, coarsely
   shredded

8 oz. carrots, peeled and
   sliced
salt and pepper
flour
chopped parsley (optional)

METHOD

1   Cut the stewing steak into fairly large cubes (the butcher may do this for you).
2   Using a medium-sized saucepan with a tightly fitting lid put in:
    (a) a layer of cabbage and carrots
    (b) a little seasoning and a good sprinkling of flour
    (c) a few pieces of meat
    (d) a little seasoning and a good sprinkling of flour.
3   Continue to add layers of vegetables and meat, sprinkling each layer with seasoning and flour.
4   When all the meat and vegetables have been used up, less than half-cover with water.
5   Put the lid on the pan and simmer for about 1 hour 30 minutes, stirring occasionally to prevent sticking.
6   Serve sprinkled with parsley if you like.

Notes: This is just as good – if not better – thoroughly reheated again for a second meal next day.

For a cheaper stew, instead of the stewing steak use a *meaty breast of lamb*, well trimmed of excess fat and cut into good-sized strips. (The butcher may first bone this for you; if not, ask him to chop it so that you can cut it easily into strips, and cook it with the bones in.) This lamb and cabbage stew is particularly popular in Norway.

Meatballs

Serves 1, or for 2 servings double the quantities
Cooking time: 1 hour

INGREDIENTS

4 oz. minced beef
half a slice of bread with
   crust removed
salt and pepper and nutmeg
chopped parsley (optional)
half an egg*

a little flour
dripping
1 small onion, finely
   chopped
stock or – better still –
   canned tomato juice

* Use the other half to add to scrambled egg, or make LAZY
SOUP (see page 14).

METHOD

1   In a bowl, break up the minced meat with a fork.
2   Soak the bread in water for a minute or two, then
   squeeze it as dry as possible and fork it into the meat.
   Season well with salt, pepper, nutmeg and chopped
   parsley.
3   Beat the egg lightly and add to the mixture, mixing
   very well. Form into 3 small cakes and dip in flour.
4   Heat some dripping in a saucepan and fry the meat-
   balls on both sides until browned on the outside.
5   Remove from the pan and in the same fat lightly fry the
   chopped onion. Sprinkle over this a dessertspoon of
   flour and mix well.
6   Return meat to pan and pour in stock or tomato juice
   almost to cover meat, add a little salt and simmer,
   covered, for an hour.

Pilaff

Serves 1–2
Small pieces of cooked rabbit, lean lamb or chicken can be
turned into an attractive pilaff.

INGREDIENTS

1 large tomato, peeled (for
   method, see page 55)
1 oz. margarine
2 oz. long-grain rice
½ teacup stock (may be
   made with vegetable
   extract or stock cube)

½ teacup milk
1 teacup diced cooked
   rabbit, lamb or chicken
seasoning
1 egg, size 4, beaten

METHOD

1   Fry the sliced tomato in the margarine.
2   Add the rice and toss for a minute or so in the tomato
    mixture.
3   Add the stock and the milk, and bring slowly to the
    boil, stirring well. Cook gently until the rice is nearly
    soft. Add the meat and seasoning and heat gently.
4   Just before serving stir in the beaten egg.

Pork and Apple Slices

Serves 2 – or, for one serving, use 1 chop and a small apple
without altering the rest of the ingredients.
Oven temperature: 400°F, 200°C, gas mark 6
Cooking time: 30 minutes

INGREDIENTS

2 pork chops
a pinch of salt
1 tablespoon lemon juice
½ teaspoon brown sugar
1 teaspoon dry mustard

a pinch of garlic powder, if
  liked
1 sliced medium cooking
  apple

METHOD 1

Baking

1   Trim the chops, and place in a greased ovenproof dish.
2   Blend the salt, lemon juice, sugar, mustard and garlic
    powder and pour over the chops.
3   Bake in a pre-heated oven at 400°F, 200°C, gas mark 6
    for 15 minutes.
4   Top the chops with the apple slices, baste well and
    bake for a further 15 minutes.

METHOD 2

Grilling

1   Trim chops and place in a greased shallow flameproof
    casserole, or the grill pan.
2   Heat the grill, lower the temperature to medium, grill
    the chops for 15 minutes on one side. Remove from the
    heat and turn the chops.

3   Blend the salt, lemon juice, sugar, mustard and garlic
    powder and pour over the chops. Top with sliced apple,
    and return to heat for a further 15 minutes.
       Be sure the apple slices do not brown too fast; baste if
    required.

Risotto

Risotto can equally well use up left-over cooked chicken, beef or lamb. Several of the ingredients can be 'optional'. For example, leave out the mushrooms or the bacon (or substitute a slice of cooked ham); add cut up tomatoes instead of peas, or else use a small can of vegetables. Dried onion can replace the peeled, chopped fresh onion. In other words, this is what I call a good-natured adaptable recipe.

Serves 2–3
Cooking time: 25 minutes

INGREDIENTS

1 oz. margarine
1 small onion, peeled and chopped (or use dried onion)
2 oz. mushrooms, washed and chopped
3 oz. long-grain rice
2 oz. streaky bacon, chopped

½ pint of chicken stock, from steamed chicken (or water and half a stock cube)
salt and pepper, to taste
tomato purée, optional
1 small packet of peas (frozen or dried)
6 oz. cooked chicken, beef or lamb, cut into pieces

METHOD

1   Melt the margarine and fry the chopped fresh onion (if used), mushrooms, rice and bacon for 5–8 minutes over gentle heat in a medium saucepan.
2   Add the stock, dried onion (if used) and seasonings, stir well and bring to the boil and simmer with the lid on the pan for 20–25 minutes, adding a little tomato

purée (optional) to give colour, and stirring occasionally.
3   Cook the peas separately, but do not overcook.
4   Meanwhile, stir in the chicken or other meat and thoroughly reheat. Add the peas. Serve hot.

Small Roasting Joints

For small roasting joints it is best to choose boneless cuts of beef, lamb or pork. Ask the butcher to cut and tie the joint so that it will keep a trim shape during roasting.

If pre-packed, follow the label instructions for timings and temperatures.

Serves 4: two portions hot one day, two portions cold next day.
Weight: about 1½–2 lb.
Oven temperature: 350°F, 180°C, gas mark 4

METHOD

1   Pre-heat the oven to 350°F, 180°C, gas mark 4. This temperature prevents excessive shrinkage.
2   Place the seasoned joint in a roasting tin with a small amount of dripping or lard. Baste the joint occasionally during cooking.
3   For rare/medium beef allow 20–25 minutes/lb plus an extra 20–25 minutes.
    For well-done beef allow 30 minutes/lb plus an extra 30 minutes.
    For lamb allow 35 minutes/lb plus an extra 35 minutes.
    For pork allow 35 minutes/lb plus an extra 35 minutes.

Steak Pan Pudding

Comment from Harlow Technical College classes: 'Students cut the cooking time of the meat by using small tins of savoury mince in place of the stewing steak. They cooked the vegetables first but omitted the onion. No difficulties in preparation, all thought the one saucepan idea a good one. They really enjoyed the pudding.'

Serves 2
Cooking time: 1 hour 30 minutes
You will need a small (2-pint) saucepan with a tightly fitting lid.

INGREDIENTS

8 oz. cubed stewing steak
1 small onion, peeled and chopped
2 carrots, peeled and sliced
1 small turnip (optional), peeled and sliced
1 oz. lard
1 tablespoon plain flour
½ pint of beef stock (use ½ beef stock cube in ½ pint of water)
salt and pepper

Pastry
3 oz. self-raising flour
3 rounded tablespoons packet shredded suet
pinch of salt
about 3 tablespoons of water to mix

METHOD

1   Brown the meat and lightly fry the onion, carrot and turnip in the melted lard.
2   Stir in the flour and cook for one minute.

3   Gradually add the stock, stirring all the time, bring to the boil and season.
4   Cover and simmer for one hour.
5   Meanwhile, mix together the pastry ingredients to form a firm dough.
6   Roll or pat out the pastry to a circle the size of the top of the pan.
7   Place the pastry lid on the contents of the pan, replace saucepan lid and simmer for a further 30 minutes until the pastry has risen and cooked.
8   Serve hot straight from the pan.

Stew and Dumplings

From Polytechnic of North London students of Home Economics.

Serves 2
Cooking time: about 1 hour 10 minutes
An economical cut of meat cooked with vegetables and stock makes a well-flavoured gravy in which the dumplings are cooked. The dish is easy to make and needs only one pan.

INGREDIENTS

1 tablespoon oil
4 oz. stewing steak, cubed
1 carrot, sliced
1 medium potato, sliced
1 small onion, sliced
1 small turnip, cubed
1 tablespoon flour
½ pint stock or water
seasoning

Dumplings
2 tablespoons self-raising
   flour
1 tablespoon packet
   shredded suet
1–2 tablespoons water
a large pinch of mixed herbs
a pinch of salt

METHOD

1 Brown the meat in hot oil in a medium-sized saucepan, then add the vegetables and cook, stirring, to brown lightly.
2 Stir in the flour, then gradually mix in the liquid and seasoning to taste. Cook, stirring all the time, for 2–3 minutes until thickened.
3 Cover and cook over a very low heat for 45 minutes, stirring occasionally.

4   Mix the dumpling ingredients together, then spoon it
     in four equal portions on top of the stew. Cover the pan
     again and simmer for a further 20 minutes. Serve
     immediately.

Note: If the stock reduces too much during the cooking of
the meat, pour in a little more before the dumplings are
added.

Steak and Kidney Crumble

This is easier to make than a steak and kidney pie.

Serves 2
Oven temperature: 325°F, 160°C, gas mark 3 raised to
350°F, 180°C, gas mark 4
Cooking time: about 2 hours or a little longer

INGREDIENTS

8 oz. stewing steak
2–3 oz. kidney
seasoned flour – about 1
    tablespoon flour mixed
    with salt and pepper

2 medium onions
crumble mixture (4 oz. flour,
    2 oz. fat)

METHOD

1   Rinse the kidney under running cold water. Trim
    surplus fat off the steak. Cut up the steak and kidney
    and coat with seasoned flour.
2   Pack into a small casserole with the sliced onion. Pour
    over about 1 teacup of water.
3   Put the lid on the casserole and bake at 325°F, 160°C,
    gas mark 3 for 1 hour 30 minutes.
4   Make a crumble with 4 oz. flour and 2 oz. fat – rub fat
    and flour together as for pastry until crumbly (or use
    6 oz. ready-mix crumble, see page 245).
5   Put the crumble mixture on top of the steak and
    kidney. Bake in the oven with the lid off at 350°F,
    180°C, gas mark 4 until crumble is brown (at least
    30–40 minutes).
        This dish can be served hot or cold.

Swiss Steak

Serves 2
Cooking braising steak in one piece is an easy way to produce a tasty and economical dish. It can be cooked in a frying pan or a saucepan.
Cooking time: about 1 hour 15 minutes

INGREDIENTS

2 tablespoons oil
1 clove garlic, peeled and
  crushed
1 medium onion, thinly
  sliced

8–10-oz. piece braising steak
2 tablespoons seasoned flour
a pinch of dried marjoram or
  thyme
a 14-oz. can tomatoes

METHOD

1   Heat the oil in a frying pan or saucepan and use to brown lightly the garlic and onion.
2   Rub the seasoned flour and the herbs into the meat on both sides.
3   Lay the meat on top of the onions and garlic. Pour the tomatoes and their juice over the meat, breaking up the tomatoes.
4   Cover and simmer very gently for about 1 hour 15 minutes, until tender. Half-way through the cooking, turn the meat and onions over to let the liquid get underneath.

Note: Mushrooms and red peppers make a good addition to this dish.

Fork-mix Pastry

Use for pies, tarts, sweet or savoury flans

INGREDIENTS

2½ oz. soft margarine or   1 tablespoon water
soft-blend white vegetable   4 oz. plain flour, sieved
fat*

* You may prefer to substitute 1 oz. low cholesterol white fat
plus 1 oz. low cholesterol margarine.

METHOD

1 Place margarine or white fat, water and 2 tablespoons
   of the flour into a bowl. Cream together with a fork
   until well mixed.
2 Stir in remaining flour to form a firm dough. Knead on
   a lightly floured surface until smooth.
3 Cover and chill if possible.

Baked Apple with Amber Sauce

Comment from teacher at Harlow Technical College: 'All
were surprised that no sugar needed to be added to the
apple'; but the class at Almondbury Further Education
Centre liked the addition of dried fruit for a little extra
sweetness.

Serves 1
Oven temperature: 350°F, 180°C, gas mark 4
Cooking time: 40 minutes to 1 hour

INGREDIENTS

1 medium cooking apple
2 cloves (optional)
3 or 4 tablespoons water
1 teaspoon lemon juice

1 tablespoon honey
sultanas, raisins, sweet
   mincemeat or chopped
   dates (optional)

METHOD

1   Core the whole unpeeled apple with corer or knife.
2   Slit the skin with a pointed knife right round the
    centre of the apple to prevent it bursting. Push a couple
    of cloves into the apple.
3   Place in an ovenproof dish. Add the water. (If you have
    a 'sweet tooth', put sultanas, raisins, sweet mincemeat
    or chopped dates into the hole left by removal of the
    core.)
4   Bake in a moderate oven (350°F, 180°C, gas mark 4)
    until the apple is soft. This may take anything from 40
    minutes to 1 hour, depending on the variety of apple.
5   Stir together the lemon juice and honey.
6   Pour the mixture over the apple when removed from
    the oven, and serve.

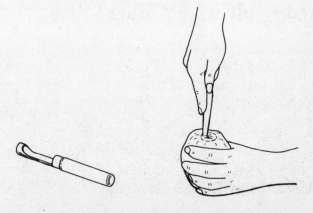

Blackcurrant Pudding

The creaminess of this pudding contrasts pleasantly with the sharpness of the blackcurrants. A quick way to serve plenty of nourishment.

Serves 2
Cooking time: a few minutes

INGREDIENTS

1 small can blackcurrants
a quarter of a packet
   blackcurrant jelly

a 5-oz. carton plain yogurt
1 tablespoon lemon juice

METHOD

1   Drain the fruit and heat the juice to just under boiling point.
2   Dissolve the jelly in heated fruit juice. Allow to cool slightly.
3   Whisk this with the yogurt and lemon juice.
4   Allow partially to set, mix in the fruit and turn into a serving dish. Serve cold.

Fruit Compote

I tasted this first in New Zealand after we had picked fresh figs and apples from the trees in a friend's garden ... Without the luxury of fresh, sun-warm figs, pears make an acceptable substitute. This can be a good recipe for using up windfalls and was known in the family as 'June's compost'!

Serves 2. Can be eaten hot one day, cold the next.
Cooking time: 10–15 minutes

INGREDIENTS

Syrup
8 fl. oz. (1 teacup) water
2 oz. (4–5 tablespoons) dark demerara or soft dark brown sugar

Fruit
2 medium cooking apples or 2–3 dessert apples
2 firm pears
1–2 tablespoons chopped dates
1–2 tablespoons raisins

METHOD

1 In a saucepan, over a gentle heat, dissolve the sugar in water and bring to the boil.
2 Peel, core and cut the fresh fruit into cubes or thick slices.
3 Simmer, together with the dried fruit, until the apples and pears are tender.

Lemon Suet Pudding

Serves 2–3
Cooking time: 2–2½ hours
You need a small (1-pint) pudding basin

INGREDIENTS

4 oz. self-raising flour
2 oz. of packet shredded suet
a pinch of salt
milk for mixing

1 lemon – juicy and
   thin-skinned
3 tablespoons golden syrup

METHOD

1   Mix together the flour, suet and salt.
2   Add sufficient milk to make a firm dough.
3   Roll out three quarters of the dough and line a greased
    1-pint pudding basin.
4   Grate the lemon rind and mix with the syrup.
5   Discard the pith from the lemon.
6   Place the whole lemon in the centre of the basin.
7   Surround with the syrup and place suet-crust lid on
    top, sealing edges firmly (first damp with a little water
    to make edges easy to seal).
8   Cover securely with foil and steam or boil for 2–2½
    hours.

Note: The lemon disintegrates during cooking, making a
gorgeously tangy, syrupy pudding. If you wish, cut the
lemon in half to remove the pips before cooking.

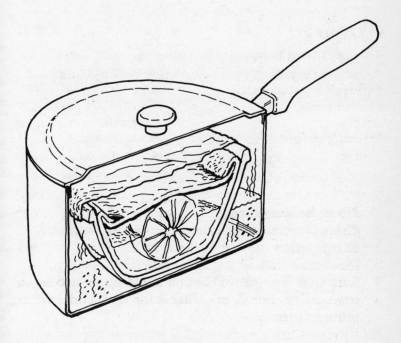

Orange Cabinet Pudding

Serves 2 – or 1 serving hot, 1 serving cold next day
Oven temperature: 350°F, 180°C, gas mark 4
Cooking time: approximately 25 minutes

INGREDIENTS

one and a half trifle sponge
   cakes, cut in half
4 glacé cherries, cut in half
a few sultanas
either
3 tablespoons carton orange
   juice

or
the juice of 1 medium
   orange

¼ pint of milk
1 large egg (beaten)
1 tablespoon sugar

METHOD

1   Place the sponge cakes in a small greased ovenproof
dish and sprinkle with glacé cherries and sultanas.
2   Beat together the orange juice, milk and egg, and add
the sugar.
3   Pour over the sponge cakes and place the dish in an
oven, 350°F, 180°C, gas mark 4 for approximately 25
minutes or until set.

Note: Add a topping of cream to this when cold and you
turn it into a trifle.

Fruity Pan Pudding

Serves 4 – 2 servings one day, reheated the second day*
Cooking time: 30 minutes
You will need a small (2-pint) saucepan with a tightly fitting lid.

INGREDIENTS

a 10- or 15-oz can of fruit
4 tablespoons water

Pastry
3 oz. self-raising flour
3 rounded tablespoons of packet shredded suet

pinch of salt
1 oz. caster sugar
¼ teaspoon ground cinnamon or mixed spice (optional)
about 3 tablespoons milk

METHOD

1   Place the canned fruit with its juice with the extra water in a saucepan and heat to simmering point.
2   Mix together pastry ingredients to form a firm dough.
3   Roll or pat out pastry to a circle the size of the top of the pan.
4   Place the pastry lid on the contents of the pan. Replace saucepan lid and simmer for 30 minutes until the pastry has risen and cooked. Serve hot straight from the pan.

*   To reheat on the second day, it is best to break up the suet crust like small dumplings so that they will heat through quickly. You may find it necessary to add more liquid, e.g., water flavoured with vitamin C blackcurrant drink.

Plum/Prune Betty

Serves 1–2
Oven temperature: 375°F, 190°C, gas mark 5
Cooking time: 45 minutes

INGREDIENTS

8 oz. plums, halved and
  stoned
2 oz. soft brown sugar
1½ tablespoons water

2 thick slices wholemeal
  bread
1 tablespoon thick honey
½ oz. margarine

This can be served with vanilla ice-cream.

METHOD

1   Stew the plums slowly with the sugar and water till soft – about 5 minutes. Allow to cool.
2   Cut the crustless bread into three-quarter-inch cubes.
3   Place half the plums in the bottom of a small oven-proof dish. Cover with a layer of bread cubes.
4   Repeat the layers once more.
5   Drizzle the honey all over the bread and dot with margarine.
6   Bake at 375°F, 190°C, gas mark 5 for about 45 minutes, until the bread is crisp and golden.

Store-cupboard alternative: Instead of fresh plums, use a small can of plums or prunes (with stones removed), plus half the juice in the can. There is no need to pre-cook – merely layer them with the bread as in the recipe above, and continue with steps 5 and 6.

Sweet Sandwich Puddings

Either left-over or freshly made sandwiches can be turned into delicious puddings.

Orange Marmalade Sandwich Pudding

Serves 1–2: serve hot, but any left over can be eaten cold later
Oven temperature: 350°F, 180°C, gas mark 4
Cooking time: 30 minutes

INGREDIENTS

2 tablespoons canned
  mandarin orange
  segments
2 slices wholemeal bread
butter or margarine

1 tablespoon marmalade
1 egg
just under ¼ pint of milk (6
  tablespoons)
demerara sugar (optional)

METHOD

1   Spoon the mandarin oranges (drained from the juice) into a small ovenproof dish.
2   Make a marmalade sandwich, cut off the crusts, then cut into squares or strips and place on top of the segments.
3   In a jug or bowl, beat the egg thoroughly with a fork. Add the milk and beat again.
4   Pour over the sandwiches. If liked, sprinkle with a little demerara sugar.
5   Bake until the custard is set, in a moderate oven (350°F, 180°C, gas mark 4) for about 30 minutes.

Notes: There is no need to grease the dish.

Broken mandarin segments are just as good as whole, and sometimes cheaper.

Other fruit, e.g. stewed rhubarb, can replace the mandarin oranges.

Rhubarb with Orange Juice

Serves 2–3

INGREDIENTS

¾–1 lb. rhubarb
3 oz. caster or brown sugar
finely grated rind and juice
  of 1 orange

a pinch of ground ginger
a few tablespoons water

Good served hot or cold, with custard or cream.

METHOD

1 Wash and trim the rhubarb. Throw away the leaves.
2 Cut the rhubarb into pieces, and place in a saucepan with the rest of the ingredients.
3 Cover and cook until tender, adding a little more water if needed.

Wholemeal Fruit Tartlets

Makes 6 individual tartlets (approx 2½ inches)
Oven temperature: 400°F, 200°C, gas mark 6
Cooking time: 15–20 minutes

INGREDIENTS

Pastry
2 oz. plain flour, mixed with
2 oz. wholemeal flour
2½ oz. soft margarine
1 tablespoon water

Filling
2 oz. curd cheese
half a small carton of peach
   yogurt
1–2 peaches, sliced (fresh or
   canned)

METHOD

1 Place about one third of the flours with the margarine and water in a mixing bowl. Cream with a fork until well blended and add the remaining flour, mixing well.

2 Knead into a firm dough on a lightly floured surface.

3 Chill the pastry and then roll it out and cut to line the tartlet tins.

4 Bake without filling in a pre-heated oven at 400°F, 200°C, gas mark 6 for 15–20 minutes.

5 When cold, mix the cheese and yogurt and fill the tartlets. Arrange the peach slices over the cheese filling.

Note: If preferred, the pastry can be cut to fit individual Yorkshire pudding tins or it can be baked on old china saucers (see SAUCER PIES, p. 183).

Date and Cherry Loaf (One-stage Method)

Oven temperature: 325°F, 160°C, gas mark 3
Cooking time: 1–1¼ hours
You will need a 1lb. loaf tin (non-stick *or* greased and base-lined)

INGREDIENTS

Cake

2 oz. soft margarine
6 oz. plain flour, sieved with
   ¼ teaspoon bicarbonate of
   soda and ½ teaspoon baking
   powder
1½ tablespoons golden
   syrup
1½ tablespoons black
   treacle

3 oz. dates and walnuts,
   chopped*
1 oz. glacé cherries, chopped
4 tablespoons milk

Decoration
icing sugar, cherries,
   angelica (optional)

* Chop 2 oz. dates with 1 oz. dried walnuts, or buy ready-mixed.

METHOD

1   Place all the cake ingredients in a bowl and beat together until well mixed (1–2 minutes).
2   Transfer to the prepared tin.
3   Bake on the middle shelf at 325°F, 160°C, gas mark 3, for 1–1¼ hours.
4   Turn out and cool on a wire tray.
5   When cold sprinkle heavily with icing sugar and place under a hot grill to melt for 1 minute. Decorate with cherries and angelica.

Date and Lemon Flapjacks

Makes 16 biscuits
Oven temperature: 350°F, 180°C, gas mark 4
Cooking time: 15–20 minutes

INGREDIENTS

3 oz. hard margarine
1 oz. soft brown sugar
2 oz. golden syrup (2 level
    tablespoons)
6 oz. rolled oats

3 oz. dates, stoned and
    chopped*
finely grated rind of 1
    lemon

* These can be bought in a packet, ready-chopped for
convenience.

METHOD

1   Melt the margarine, sugar and syrup in a saucepan over
    low heat until all the sugar is dissolving.
2   Remove from heat and stir in the rolled oats, chopped
    dates and lemon rind.
3   Press the mixture into a greased oblong tin, approxi-
    mately 10 × 7 inches. Smooth the top with the back of
    a spoon.
4   Bake at 350°F, 180°C, gas mark 4 for – about 20
    minutes. Cut down into 4 strips and then across into 4,
    to make 16 biscuits. Leave in the tin until cold.

Lemon Cake

Oven temperature: 350°F, 180°C, gas mark 4
Cooking time: approximately 45 minutes

INGREDIENTS

Cake
4 oz. soft margarine
4 oz. caster sugar
2 eggs, size 1 or 2
1 tablespoon milk
4 oz. self-raising flour ⎫
1 level teaspoon   ⎬ sieved together
   baking powder   ⎭

grated rind of 1 lemon

Lemon Syrup
2 oz. caster sugar
juice of 1 lemon

METHOD

1   Grease and line the base of a 7-inch cake tin using greased greaseproof paper or ungreased baking parchment.
2   Place all cake ingredients in mixing bowl and beat with a wooden spoon until the mixture is smooth, 2–3 minutes.
3   Place in cake tin and bake on the middle shelf of a moderate oven, 350°F, 180°C, gas mark 4, for approximately 45 minutes.
4   When the cake is baked – when it is firm to a light finger-touch, and just shrunk away from the side of the tin – turn it out on to the cooling tray, remove the paper, and leave upside-down.

5   Make the lemon syrup by dissolving the caster sugar in
    the juice of the lemon over gentle heat and boiling it
    for one minute.
6   With the bottom of the cake uppermost, make three or
    four slits with a sharp knife, and pour the warm syrup
    into the warm cake.
7   When cool, reverse the cake and dust with sieved icing
    sugar.

Shortcake Sandwich

Serves 4 – for 8 servings, double the ingredients and make the shortcake in two 7-inch sandwich tins. The two whole cakes are then sandwiched together and topped with the fruit and cream.
Oven temperature: 325°F, 160°C, gas mark 3
Cooking time: 35–40 minutes

INGREDIENTS

2 oz. soft margarine
2 oz. caster sugar
2 oz. semolina
2 oz. self-raising flour,
    sieved with ½ teaspoon
    baking powder
1 egg, size 3
¼ teaspoon almond essence

Filling
1 tablespoon strawberry jam

Topping
canned or fresh fruit
    e.g. strawberries, peaches,
    kiwi fruit
¼ pint of double cream,
    whipped

METHOD

1 Grease and base-line a 7-inch sandwich tin.
2 Place all the cake ingredients in a bowl and beat together until well mixed, 2–3 minutes.
3 Spread into the prepared tin.
4 Bake on the middle shelf of a pre-heated oven at 325°F, 160°C, gas mark 3 for 35–40 minutes.
5 Turn out to cool on a wire tray, removing the paper.
6 When cold, cut in half, making 2 semi-circles. Sandwich these together with jam, cut into 4 slices and top with strawberries and cream.

Potato Scones

Next time you are preparing mashed potatoes, you may like to make some extra for these delicious Potato Scones.

Serve hot, sliced and buttered for tea, or as a pudding with golden syrup.

Makes 8
Oven temperature: 400°F, 200°C, gas mark 6
Cooking time: 15 minutes

INGREDIENTS

4 oz. self-raising flour
2 oz. packet shredded suet
a pinch of salt
4 oz. cold mashed potato

1 tablespoon caster sugar
1 tablespoon currants
1 tablespoon sultanas
milk for mixing

METHOD

1   Mix together all ingredients with sufficient milk to make a stiff dough.
2   Roll out to half an inch thick and cut out 8 rounds using a 2-inch plain cutter.
3   Brush with milk.
4   Place on greased baking sheet and bake at 400°F, 200°C, gas mark 6 for about 15 minutes.

Wholemeal Scones

Makes 8–10
Oven temperature: 425°F, 220°C, gas mark 7
Cooking time: 12–15 minutes

INGREDIENTS

9 oz. wholemeal flour
pinch of salt
4 teaspoons baking powder

2 oz. butter or margarine
approx. ¼ pint of milk

METHOD

1   Place the flour, salt and baking powder in a bowl and rub in the butter or margarine until the mixture resembles fine breadcrumbs.
2   Add the milk and mix to a soft dough. Turn on to a floured surface and knead until smooth.
3   Roll out to three quarters of an inch thick. Using a 2-inch cutter make 8–10 scones.
4   Place on a greased baking tray, brush with extra milk and bake in a pre-heated oven at 425°F, 220°C, gas mark 7 for 12–15 minutes.
5   Cool on a wire rack or serve warm, split and buttered.

Variations

1   For a lighter scone, replace 2 oz. of the wholemeal flour with 2 oz. plain white flour.
2   For a savoury scone add 2 oz. grated Cheddar cheese and ½ teaspoon mustard.
3   For a sweet scone add 2 oz. sultanas, currants or raisins and ½–1 tablespoon caster sugar (optional).

Chapter 4

Favourites from the Cookery Classes

Contents

When *Easy Cooking for One or Two* was first published in 1972 one of its aims was to provide a selection of tested recipes for newly formed 'Retirement' or 'Over-sixties' cookery classes. In return, once the class had tried out the recipes, the teacher filled in a questionnaire answering the following:

1. Did they find the recipe easy to make?
2. Did they enjoy it?
3. Would they make it again at home?

Only when the answer to all three questions was 'yes' did the recipe find a place in the book.

In revising this chapter some fifteen years later, I decided to contact again as many of those classes as possible. The teachers had changed and, alas, some of the classes had closed, but the rest of the classes were coping with present-day problems in a most imaginative and practical manner.

Some teachers have sent notes and articles about their work, as well as their favourite recipes for me to cook for this chapter. From Dorrie Smith I had details of the Cookery for Men class. This is open to married men whose wives are convalescing or invalids, as well as bachelors and widowers, including those already retired from work. The local hospital service also sends along to this class male patients who have to live alone on returning home.

Valerie Goulding described similar classes run for men and women who join for social reasons as well as practical ones: housewives, retired pensioners and others anxious to learn in congenial company how to budget, shop and cook for one or two. Karin Mitchell gave many details about cookery classes run for those who are visually disabled; there are other classes for those with physical or mental difficulties. Lucille Barber and Elna Forsyth described recipes to demonstrate cooking techniques.

There are classes for one-parent families in difficult social conditions. Some classes cater especially for employees made redundant.

This chapter includes recipes popular with men and women in their seventies, eighties and nineties, who are being encouraged to retain an interest in food by tasting the dishes at a luncheon club; Stephanie Baldwin told me of classes for those in sheltered accommodation.

Classes are being run in rural areas as well as towns, and their teachers include home economists and dietitians making sure that the food is nourishing as well as tempting. For details of classes in your area, apply to your local library or Town Hall. If none exists, a letter to a local newspaper could stir up interest.

May I say a grateful thank you to all the teachers and students who sent me recipes to include in this book. The names of their classes – past and present – are listed below:

Almondbury Further Education Centre, Arbroath, Angus; Barnet College of Further Education (Sheltered Accommodation); Basford Hall College of Further Education (Luncheon Club Class); Bedale Agricultural Centre (Cooking for One or Two); Braunstone Adult Education Centre, Leicester; Camden Institute, London; Charles Keene College of Further Education, Leicester; Coventry Technical College; The Elms Technical College, Stoke-on-Trent; Fulham and South Kensington Institute (Pensioners' Luncheon Club); Harlow Technical College; Hounslow Borough College; North Riding of Yorkshire Rural Economics Service; Polytechnic of North London (Students of Home Economics); Richmond Adult and Community College (Cookery for the Visually Disabled, and the Lunch Club Class); Sheffield Polytechnic; South Manchester Community College, Wythenshawe (Everyday Cookery, including Retirement); Swinton Adult Education Centre (Cookery for Men); Wolverhampton College of Adult Education (Cookery Class).

Potato and Milk Soup

Serves 2
Cooking time: 20–30 minutes

INGREDIENTS

½ pint of milk
1 medium raw potato
half a small onion (or 1
   teaspoon dried onion)

salt and pepper
2 tablespoons grated cheese
chopped parsley (optional)

METHOD

1   Put the milk into a saucepan.
2   Peel the potato and fresh onion and grate into the milk
    (or add dried onion to avoid grating fresh onion).
3   Simmer gently until tender, 20–30 minutes.
4   Add seasoning to taste.
5   Serve sprinkled with grated cheese and parsley.

Alternative suggestions:

Grate extra vegetables to give additional flavour and to
make a vegetable soup.
Sieve the cooked soup for a smoother texture.

Leek and Macaroni Gratin

Serves 1
Oven temperature: 375°F, 190°C, gas mark 5
Cooking time: 30–35 minutes, after preparation time

INGREDIENTS

1 oz. short-cut macaroni
   (plain or wholemeal)
1 small leek
½ oz. butter or margarine
½ tablespoon plain flour
¼ pint of milk

1½ oz. grated Cheddar
   cheese
salt and pepper
½ oz. bread, in crumbs or
   small cubes
a few fresh or dried chives

Serve decorated with wedges of tomato.

METHOD

1   Cook the macaroni in boiling salted water until just
    tender following packet instructions. Drain.
2   Trim the leek, cut lengthwise to wash, then slice very
    thinly.
3   Melt butter in the saucepan and sauté the leek for 2
    minutes. Add flour and stir to cook for 1 minute.
4   Remove from the heat, add the milk gradually, then
    bring slowly back to the boil, stirring.
5   Add the macaroni and about two thirds of the cheese.
    Season with salt and pepper. Pour into a greased oven-
    proof dish.
6   Mix the bread, the rest of the cheese and the chives and
    sprinkle on top.
7   Bake at 375°F, 190°C, gas mark 5 for 30–35 minutes
    until the top is golden brown.

Potato and Cheese Savoury Custard

Comment from the classes: 'This is a great favourite. The cooked bacon gives an added flavour, and the whole dish is tasty.

'One student told me afterwards it had given her the idea of using up other vegetables, and she had used cooked carrots instead of potatoes; she was very satisfied with the result and was pleased with the idea of experimenting with other vegetables.'

Serves 2
Oven temperature: 325°F, 160°C, gas mark 3
Cooking time: 40 minutes

INGREDIENTS

margarine or butter
2 rashers cooked bacon,
or 1 oz. cooked ham
8 oz. cooked sliced potato

2 oz. grated Cheddar cheese
1 egg, large
½ pint of milk
salt and pepper

METHOD

1   Grease an ovenproof dish with margarine or butter.
2   Chop the bacon or ham.
3   Place in the dish in layers: potato, cheese, bacon, potato, cheese.
4   Beat the egg, add the milk and seasoning, pour over the layers in the dish.
5   Bake, uncovered, at 325°F, 160°C, gas mark 3 for 40 minutes or until the custard is set.

Salad in a Bowl

Serves 1

INGREDIENTS

Dressing
2 teaspoons oil
1 teaspoon vinegar or lemon
   juice
salt, pepper, mustard, sugar

Base (cold cooked ingredients)
cooked potato
or cooked pasta
or cooked rice
or canned butter beans,
   drained

Salad vegetables
Choose 2 or 3 varieties e.g.,
lettuce
watercress
cucumber
celery
carrots
tomatoes
bean sprouts
spring onions

Serve with
sliced meat (e.g., tongue,
   ham)
or hard-boiled egg
or canned pilchards, sardines
   or tuna

METHOD

1   In a small serving bowl, fork together the ingredients
    for the dressing, adding a pinch of each of the season-
    ings to flavour to your taste.
2   Toss the chosen base ingredient in this dressing to
    moisten.
3   Chop up the salad vegetables and stir in lightly.
4   Decorate with strips of meat, sliced egg or flaked fish.

Tuna Bake

Serves 2 – or 1 hot, 1 cold serving
Oven temperature: 350°F, 180°C, gas mark 4
or a medium grill for heating through after preparation

INGREDIENTS

1 small packet crisps
1–2 oz. grated Cheddar
  cheese
¼ pint of white sauce*
1 small can tuna fish, drained
  and flaked

1 hard-boiled egg, chopped
chopped parsley and lemon
  juice to taste
salt and pepper
a green vegetable or salad
wholemeal bread

* Either use a packet sauce mix, or a home-made sauce using
¼ pint of milk to ½ oz. margarine and ½ oz. plain flour (for
method see page 57).

METHOD

1 Crush the crisps and mix with some of the grated
  cheese.
2 Make the white sauce or use a packet mix.
3 Combine the sauce, tuna, egg and the rest of the
  cheese. Add parsley, lemon juice and seasoning (taste
  to get the strength of flavour you like).
4 Place in greased baking dish.
5 Sprinkle crushed crisps and cheese on top.
6 Heat through until just bubbling in a moderate oven
  (350°F, 180°C, gas mark 4) or under the grill.
7 Serve with a vegetable or salad and wholemeal bread.

Note: The crisps are a little un-crisp by the second meal, but it still tastes delicious. If you prefer, you could put the cold portion with a few separate crisps aside at step 3, cover and keep in a cold larder till next day. Then proceed with steps 4–6 for a hot meal.

Fish with Vegetables

Serves 2
Cooking time: approximately 20 minutes

INGREDIENTS

2 or 3 carrots, peeled and
  thinly sliced
1 small onion, peeled and
  thinly sliced
2 stalks celery, thinly sliced
1 oz. butter or margarine
8 oz. fish fillet (haddock, cod
  or other white fish)

2 tomatoes, peeled (see page
  55) and chopped
1 tablespoon water
half a bay leaf
pinch of mixed herbs
1 tablespoon top of the milk
shake of pepper

METHOD

1   Cook the carrots, onion and celery gently in the fat
    until soft (this may take 10 minutes or longer with
    occasional stirring).
2   Cut fish into fairly large pieces and when the vege-
    tables are cooked, add the fish to the pan and baste
    with the vegetables. Let this cook for a minute or two.
3   Add the peeled chopped tomatoes, a tablespoon of
    water and the bay leaf and herbs.
4   Cover the pan and cook for about 10 minutes or until
    the fish is done.
5   Remove the fish to warm plates, add a tablespoon of
    the top of the milk and a shake of pepper to the
    vegetables. Stir well, and then pour the vegetable
    mixture over the fish.

Sausage Casserole

Serves 2
Oven temperature: 350°F, 180°C, gas mark 4
Cooking time: 30 minutes

INGREDIENTS

4–6 sausages
a small knob of cooking fat
1 small onion, peeled and
   chopped
2–4 oz. mushrooms, washed
   and sliced

1 *small* can (140 g) condensed
   tomato soup
1 small cooking apple,
   peeled, cored and cut into
   rings
1 dessertspoon demerara
   sugar

Serve with a green vegetable and noodles or other pasta.

METHOD

1   Prick the sausages with a fork and fry until golden
    brown in the fat. Place the sausages in a shallow
    casserole or baking dish.
2   Soften the onion and mushrooms in the fat remaining
    in the pan. Drain and add to the sausages.
3   Add the tomato soup mixed with one tin of water.
4   Place apple rings around the edge and sprinkle with the
    sugar.
5   Bake at 350°F, 180°C, gas mark 4 for about 30 minutes.

Scotch Eggs (Baked)

Scotch eggs are traditionally fried in deep fat, but this recipe from the Swinton Adult Education Centre 'Cookery for Men' class gives the less fatty, easier and safer method of baking in the oven.

Serves 2
Oven temperature: 375°F, 190°C, gas mark 5
Cooking time: 25–30 minutes

INGREDIENTS

2 eggs, hard-boiled
1 egg (use the yolk for the egg wash and the white for another recipe*)

4 oz. sausagemeat
2 oz. dry breadcrumbs (home-made or commercial)

* e.g., whisk and stir into fruit purée.

These can be eaten hot with cooked vegetables, or served cold with salad.

METHOD

1 Hard boil the eggs (10–12 minutes, according to size) and cool immediately under cold running water. Peel off the shell, then leave the eggs in cold water for 10 minutes to cool completely to stop a black ring forming round the yolk.
2 Divide the sausagemeat in half and carefully wrap round each egg.

3   Coat with beaten egg yolk and roll them in crumbs.
4   Place on a greased baking tray and bake for 25–30
    minutes at 375°F, 190°C, gas mark 5.

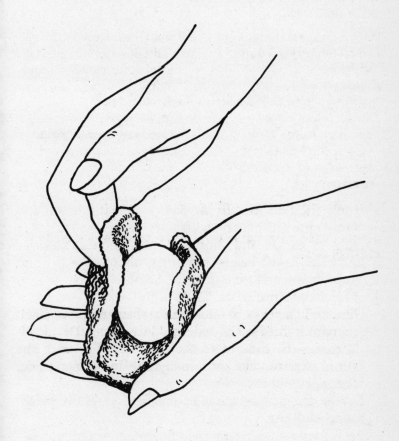

Sausage Hot-pot

Serves 2
Cooking time: approx. 30–40 minutes

INGREDIENTS

½ oz. cooking fat or lard
1 small onion, peeled and
  chopped
4 sausages
2 carrots, peeled and sliced
2 sticks celery, sliced
1 small tin baked beans

1 small can tomatoes
¼ pint of water
1 level dessertspoon tomato
  purée
salt and pepper
8 oz. potatoes
a small knob of margarine

METHOD

1 Melt the lard in a frying pan, soften the onion and brown the sausages on both sides.
2 Add the carrots and celery and cook for 5 minutes.
3 Add the baked beans, tomatoes, chopped with their juice, water and tomato purée. Season lightly.
4 Cover and simmer for 30–40 minutes.
5 Meanwhile peel and thickly slice the potatoes and boil them in lightly salted water till just tender. Drain.
6 Transfer the hot-pot to a casserole, cover with the sliced potatoes, dot with margarine and brown under the grill.

Note: To save washing up, use a flameproof casserole, i.e., one which can take the heat of a gas or electric ring and the grill.

Chicken Casserole de Luxe

Serves 2
Cooking time: approximately 1 hour

INGREDIENTS

2 chicken joints
1 oz. butter
1 medium onion, chopped
2 rashers back bacon,
   chopped
3 oz. mushrooms, sliced

1 tablespoon flour
½ pint of stock
1 tablespoon sherry
½ tablespoon tomato purée
salt and pepper

METHOD

1 Brown the chicken joints in the butter, then remove from pan.
2 Sauté the onion and bacon for about 5 minutes. Add the mushrooms and continue cooking until softened. Stir in the flour.
3 Add the stock, sherry and tomato purée to the pan slowly, off the heat, stirring.
4 Return to the heat and bring to the boil, stirring occasionally. Replace the chicken joints and simmer gently until tender, about 45 minutes to 1 hour, tasting for seasoning.

Note: This dish – made in larger quantities – was thoroughly enjoyed at the end-of-term party for the Richmond Cookery for the Visually Disabled class. A whole chicken was roasted, taken off the bone, cut up and reheated in the sauce: that made it particularly easy to eat.

Chicken Pie

Makes a substantial meal from a small amount of left-over cooked chicken.

Serves 2
Oven temperature: 400°F, 200°C, gas mark 6
Cooking time: 30 minutes, after preparation time
You will need a 6–8-inch pie dish.

INGREDIENTS

FORK-MIX PASTRY, using
6 oz. flour

Filling

1 rasher bacon, chopped
1 oz. butter
1 small onion, sliced
1 medium carrot, sliced
1 small stick of celery
  (optional)
1–2 tablespoons peas
  (optional)
2 oz. mushrooms, sliced

1 level dessertspoon
  cornflour
⅓ pint of boiling water plus
  ½ chicken stock cube
about 4–6 oz. cooked
  chicken, cut into small
  pieces
salt and pepper
beaten egg or milk to glaze

METHOD

1   Make the pastry (see page 120 if you need a reminder).
2   Fry the bacon lightly. Add the butter and sauté the onion, carrot, celery and mushrooms to soften. Remove from pan.
3   Stir the cornflour into the fat remaining in the pan and cook for 2 minutes. Remove from the heat, blend in the stock, then return to the heat and bring to the boil.

4 Add the vegetables and chicken and taste for seasoning.
5 Transfer to pie dish and cover with pastry (damp edge of dish and pastry rim). Brush with beaten egg or milk.
6 Bake at 400°F, 200°C, gas mark 6 for about 30 minutes, until the pastry is golden.

Chicken in a Parcel

Serves 1
Oven temperature: 400°F, 200°C, gas mark 6
Cooking time: 45 minutes–1 hour
You will need kitchen foil.

INGREDIENTS

1–2 chicken thigh portions
1 oz. cooking fat
or 1 tablespoon oil
1 small onion, chopped
1–2 oz. mushrooms, washed
    and sliced

1 small can tomatoes,
    drained from juice and
    chopped
pinch of mixed herbs
salt and pepper

Serve with a potato baked in its jacket (see page 64)*

METHOD

1   Lightly fry the chicken in the cooking fat or oil. Place
    on a square of foil.
2   Soften the onion and the mushrooms in the remaining
    fat. Arrange on top of the chicken.
3   Place the chopped tomatoes, herbs, salt and pepper on
    top. Fold into a loose parcel. Place on a baking tray.
4   Bake for 45 minutes–1 hour at 400°F, 200°C, gas mark
    6.

* A small 4-oz. potato will bake at this temperature and time.
A larger 6-oz. potato can be cut in half lengthwise before
baking.

Lemon Roast Chicken

Oven temperature: 400°F, 200°C, gas mark 6
Cooking time: 1 hour 15 minutes

INGREDIENTS

3 lb. roasting chicken, fresh
  or frozen (thoroughly
  defrosted)
2 lemons
1 clove garlic, crushed

1 oz. butter, softened or
  melted
2 tablespoons vegetable oil
2 tablespoons fresh parsley
  or 1 teaspoon dried

Serve hot with new potatoes and green vegetables.
Serve cold with salad; when cold the juices set to a jelly
which can be eaten with the chicken.

METHOD

1　Grate the rind from both lemons. Remove the pith from one lemon and chop the flesh. Squeeze the juice from the second lemon and save for use in step 5.
2　Mix the garlic with the lemon flesh and half the lemon rind and put inside the cavity of the bird.
3　Place the chicken in a roasting pan, rub the softened butter and the remaining lemon rind over the skin and season with salt and pepper. Pour on the oil.
4　Roast for 1 hour at 400°F, 200°C, gas mark 6, basting once or twice.
5　Pour lemon juice and sprinkle parsley over chicken, baste and replace in oven for a further 15 minutes.
6　Pour off the fat and mash the stuffing into the pan juices.
7　Place the chicken on a serving dish ready for carving. Strain the juices and serve as a gravy.

Beef in Beer

Comment from Wolverhampton College of Adult Education Cookery Class: a flavoursome sauce using the brown ale. Men's comment: what a waste of beer!

Serves 4: eat 1 or 2 portions and freeze the rest; or reheat the left-overs thoroughly for next day; or make half quantities for 2 servings.
Oven temperature: 300°F, 150°C, gas mark 2
Cooking time: 3 hours. The long, slow cooking in the beer helps to tenderize the meat.

INGREDIENTS

1 lb. shin or stewing beef
lard for frying
½ lb. onions
½ lb. carrots
2 sticks of celery

2 oz. plain flour
½ pint of brown ale
1 pint of stock
salt and pepper
bouquet garni*

* bouquet garni – a bunch of herbs tied together e.g., parsley, thyme and bay leaf, or bought dried, ready made up like a teabag, or sachet. Remove before serving.

METHOD

1   Cut the beef into cubes – your butcher may do this for you. Melt the fat in a large pan and fry the meat to seal and brown it. Remove the meat to casserole dish.
2   Peel and roughly chop the vegetables, add to the fat in the pan and toss them over the heat for a few minutes.
3   Take off the heat and stir in the flour. Add the ale and stock (this can be made from a stock cube and water).

4   Return to the heat and bring to the boil, stirring. Add a
    little salt and pepper and the bouquet garni.
5   Pour over the meat and cook, covered, in the oven for
    3 hours at 300°F, 150°C, gas mark 2.

Beef Cobbler

Serves 2
Oven temperature: 425°F, 220°C, gas mark 7
Cooking time: 1 hour–1 hour 15 minutes on top of the stove,
followed by 20 minutes in the oven

INGREDIENTS

½ oz. lard
half an onion (chopped)
6 oz. raw minced beef
1 dessertspoon flour
a teacup of cream of
    tomato soup
2–4 oz. carrots, chopped
    finely
salt and pepper

Topping
3 oz. plain flour
1½ level teaspoons baking
    powder
¼ teaspoon salt
1 oz. margarine
1½ oz. cream of tomato
    soup (about 2½
    tablespoons)
milk to glaze

METHOD

1   Melt the lard in a saucepan and fry the onion and beef
    until lightly browned. Lift out and keep on one side.
2   Stir the flour into the fat remaining in the pan, add the
    soup, stirring well to clear the bottom of the pan, and
    bring to the boil.
3   Return the meat and onions to the pan with the
    carrots. Season lightly and simmer gently for 1 hour–1
    hour 15 minutes. The pan should be covered with a lid
    but the contents should be stirred occasionally.
4   Make the topping by rubbing the margarine into the
    sieved flour, baking powder and salt; bind together
    with the tomato soup.

5   Roll out the dough to half an inch thick, cut into six or
    seven one-inch rounds, brush with milk and place on
    top of meat. Cook, with the lid off, in the oven at
    425°F, 220°C, gas mark 7 until well risen, approxi-
    mately 20 minutes.

Baked Lamb Chop

Note from Basford Hall College of Further Education: a real favourite for cooking for one. Any meat can be substituted – even liver or chicken.

Serves 1
Oven temperature: 325°F, 160°C, gas mark 3
Cooking time: 1 hour

INGREDIENTS

1 lamb chump chop
a knob of margarine or
   cooking fat
half a small onion, sliced

half a small can tomatoes, or
   2 fresh
salt and pepper
1 oz. grated cheese*
1 tablespoon breadcrumbs*

* 2 tablespoons packet stuffing could be substituted for the cheese and breadcrumbs.

METHOD

1   Brown the chop in a little fat. Put into a casserole dish.
2   Place sliced onion and tomatoes on top of chop. Season.
3   Mix grated cheese and breadcrumbs together (or use packet stuffing, dry) and sprinkle on top.
4   Cover and bake at 325°F, 160°C, gas mark 3 for 1 hour.

Note: There is no need to add any stock because the juices run out during the long, slow cooking to give plenty of liquor.

Chops in Foil

Most recipes using chops may be altered to cook the chops in a foil parcel, either singly or all together. They are served in the foil and can then be tipped onto the plate with their savoury juices. Chops wrapped in foil are deliciously tender and do not shrink nearly as much as grilled or fried chops.

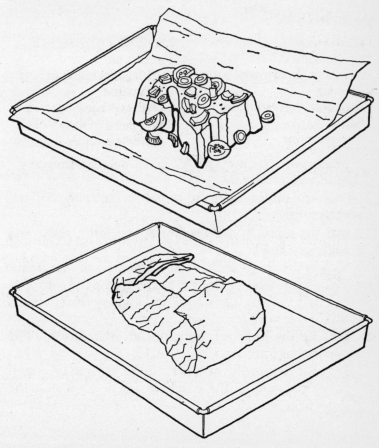

Italian Chops

Serves 2, or halve quantity for 1 person
Oven temperature: 425°F, 220°C, gas mark 7
Cooking time: 40 minutes
You will need a piece of kitchen foil 18 inches square; for 1
chop foil needs to be only 12 inches square.

INGREDIENTS

1 small onion
2 ripe tomatoes
½ teaspoon dried mixed herbs
seasoning
1 teaspoon Worcestershire
   sauce
a pinch of sugar

2 lamb chops, trimmed of
   excess fat
a small pat of butter or
   margarine
2 small scrubbed potatoes
   for baking in their jackets
   (optional)

METHOD

1   Dice the onion, skin the tomatoes (see page 55) and
    chop finely.
2   Mix the onion, tomatoes, herbs, seasoning, sauce and
    sugar in a bowl.
3   Season the chops and spread with butter or margarine.
4   Place the foil on a baking tray and grease the centre.
5   Put half the mixture on the foil and lay the chops on
    this, cover with remaining mixture.
6   Fold up the foil over the chops, overlapping ends by
    two inches forming a loose parcel.
7   Bake for 40 minutes at 425°F, 220°C, gas mark 7. Small
    baked potatoes in their jackets can be cooked at the
    same time.

Hungarian Chops

Serves 2
Cooking time: approximately 25 minutes

INGREDIENTS

2 pork chops, if possible loin
2 tablespoons butter
salt, pepper and paprika
1 small onion, finely
  chopped

1 small green pepper, sliced
1 teacup hot water
2 tomatoes, sliced
1 teaspoon flour
3 tablespoons plain yogurt

METHOD

1   Beat the chops with a rolling pin to flatten slightly.
2   Melt the butter and fry the chops until golden brown and thoroughly cooked through.
3   Season with salt, pepper and paprika, arrange on a shallow serving dish and keep hot while you make the sauce.
4   Fry the onion in the remaining juices, add the green pepper and hot water. Cover and simmer for a few minutes. Then add the tomatoes and simmer again.
5   Blend the flour with a little cold water and thicken the sauce. Bring back to simmering point. Stir in the yogurt and taste for seasoning.
6   Pour over the pork chops and serve.

Lamb Cassoulet

Serves 2 for the first meal, then reheat thoroughly for another
2 portions next day.
Oven temperature: 350°F, 180°C, gas mark 4
Cooking time: 1 hour 30 minutes

INGREDIENTS

12 oz. raw lamb, cubed
2 oz. streaky bacon
oil
1 onion
1 clove garlic (optional)
a 14-oz. can tomatoes

¼ pint of beef stock
1 can butter beans
bouquet garni (see page 160)
salt and pepper

METHOD

1   Cut the meat into cubes, or ask the butcher to do this
    for you. Chop the bacon.
2   Fry the bacon pieces in a dry pan, then remove to a
    casserole.
3   Add a little oil to the pan. Brown the meat well on all
    sides.
4   Remove to casserole (with a slotted spoon if you have
    one, to avoid transfer of oil).
5   Fry the onion and garlic until softened. Add to the
    casserole with the chopped tomatoes, juice, stock and
    drained butter beans.
6   Add bouquet garni, season lightly and bake at 350°F,
    180°C, gas mark 4 for 1 hour 30 minutes.

Lamb and Herb Hot-pot

Serves 2, or 1 portion can be reheated thoroughly for next day.
Oven temperature: 350°F, 180°C, gas mark 4, raised to
400°F, 200°C, gas mark 6
Cooking time: 1 hour 30 minutes (the last half an hour at the
higher temperature)

INGREDIENTS

oil *or* dripping
8–12 oz. best end neck or
    scrag of lamb
1 onion, sliced
1 carrot, sliced
½ tablespoon flour
⅓ pint of beef stock

1 large tablespoon tomato
    ketchup
½ teaspoon dried rosemary
    or dill
12 oz. potatoes, peeled and
    sliced
½ oz. melted butter

METHOD

1   Heat the oil or dripping and fry the pieces of lamb until
    well browned. Transfer to a casserole.
2   In the same fat, fry the onion and carrot for 2 minutes.
3   Stir in the flour and cook for 1 minute. Remove from
    the heat.
4   Gradually add the stock (which can be made with a
    stock cube) and bring to the boil, stirring frequently.
5   Add the tomato ketchup and rosemary or dill. Pour
    over the meat. The liquor should cover the meat.
6   Top with potato slices and brush with butter.
7   Bake, covered at 350°F, 180°C, gas mark 4, for 1 hour.
    Uncover and continue baking at 400°F, 200°C, gas
    mark 6 for a further 30 minutes until the potatoes are
    golden brown.

Liver Fricassée

Serves 1

INGREDIENTS

2 or 3 thin slices of lamb's or
    pig's liver
margarine

For sauce
½ oz. soft margarine
½ oz. plain flour
¼ pint of milk
seasoning
pinch mixed herbs
a little lemon juice

Garnish
chopped parsley, a wedge of
    lemon

METHOD

1   Fry the liver gently in the margarine until lightly cooked.
2   To make the sauce, put all the ingredients in a small saucepan and whisk until the sauce boils. Stir for 2–3 minutes until cooked.
3   Cut the liver into bite-size pieces, return them to the pan in which they were fried, add the sauce to this pan and heat well through.
4   Sprinkle with the roughly chopped parsley, serve with a wedge of lemon.

Note: Optional additions to this dish – a few mushrooms cooked with the liver; some peas, fresh or canned; croûtons of toast.

Meat Loaf

Notes from Richmond Cookery for the Visually Disabled Class: We found this an easy method. If you want to serve this meat loaf cold, cool before turning out. Refrigerate and serve with a green salad.

If you want to serve it hot, it can be eaten with a vegetable and jacket potatoes cooked at the same time. Tomato soup is popular poured over as a sauce when it is served hot (or make QUICK TOMATO SAUCE, page 17).

Serves 2 hot one day with 1 or 2 portions cold for next day
Oven temperature: 350°F, 180°C, gas mark 4
Cooking time: 1 hour
You will need a 1-lb. loaf tin, lightly greased, then lined with foil (or a non-stick tin)

INGREDIENTS

1 large onion, finely chopped
2 oz. chopped mushrooms
knob of butter
1½ level tablespoons flour
8 tablespoons milk
8 oz. minced beef
4 oz. pork sausage meat
½ teaspoon Worcestershire sauce
2 teaspoons chopped parsley

½ teaspoon chopped mixed herbs or
¼ teaspoon mixed dried herbs
1½ teaspoons tomato purée
1½ tablespoons porridge oats, or fresh breadcrumbs
¼ teaspoon salt, shake of pepper

METHOD

1   Fry the onion and mushrooms in the butter to soften but not brown for about 1 minute. Add flour and cook for 2 minutes.

2   Gradually add the milk off the heat, then bring to the boil. Pour into a large bowl to cool.
3   Add the remaining ingredients and mix well.
4   Put into the tin and bake for 1 hour at 350°F, 180°C, gas mark 4.

Meat Loaf (Savoury)

Comment from Wythenshawe 'Everyday Cookery (including retirement)' class: The curry flavour is only mild, but could be omitted if preferred. This meat loaf was enjoyed by all the class. In fact one student made it 3 times instead of other dishes.

Serves 4 – or 2 portions hot with green vegetables and 2 portions cold with salad.
Oven temperature: 375°F, 190°C, gas mark 5, reduced to 350°F, 180°C, gas mark 4
Cooking time: 30 minutes at the higher temperature and a further 30 minutes on the reduced heat.
You will need a 1-lb. loaf tin either well greased or, preferably, non-stick.

INGREDIENTS

2 oz. (2 large slices) bread, broken into small pieces
¼ pint of milk
a little oil
1 chopped onion
½ tablespoon vinegar or lemon juice

½ teaspoon salt
shake of pepper
½ tablespoon curry powder (optional)
1 teaspoon sugar
12 oz. minced beef
1 small egg

METHOD

1 Soak the bread in milk for about a quarter of an hour. Pour away the excess milk.
2 Meanwhile heat the oil and fry the onion until pale golden. Stir in the vinegar, salt, pepper, curry powder and sugar.

3   In a large bowl, beat the seasoned onion with the bread, and mix in the meat and egg until well combined.
4   Bake in the loaf tin for 30 minutes at 375°F, 190°C, gas mark 5; reduce heat to 350°F, 180°C, gas mark 4 and bake for a further 30 minutes.

Mushroom and Bacon Roly Poly

Serves 2
Oven temperature: 400°F, 200°C, gas mark 6
Cooking time: 35–40 minutes

INGREDIENTS

Suet pastry
4 oz. self-raising flour
1 teaspoon baking powder
2 oz. shredded suet
a good pinch of salt and
    pepper
2–3 tablespoons water

Filling
3 oz. mushrooms, finely
    chopped
2 oz. streaky bacon,
    chopped, rind removed
quarter of an onion, grated
½ teaspoon dried mixed
    herbs
a dash of lemon juice

Serve with vegetables and QUICK TOMATO SAUCE (p. 17).

METHOD

1   Mix the flour, baking powder, suet and seasoning. Make into a soft dough with the water.
2   Roll out to an oblong about 10 inches by 7 inches.
3   Mix the filling together and spread it over the pastry to within 1 inch of the edges.

4   Damp the edges and roll up, sealing the ends.
5   Wrap in greased foil and bake at 400°F, 200°C, gas mark
    6 for 35–40 minutes.

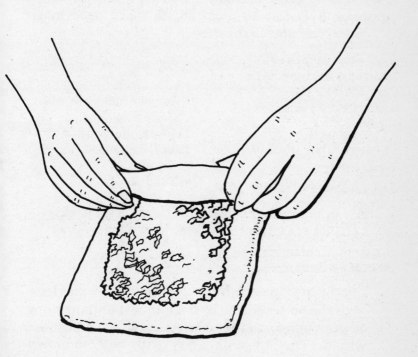

Liver in Yogurt Sauce

Serves 2

Note from Wythenshawe 'Everyday Cookery (including Retirement)' class: although this recipe asks for lamb's liver, ox liver can be used, but this will need longer cooking, preferably in the oven.

INGREDIENTS

½ lb. lamb's liver
½ oz. butter
1 teaspoon oil
1 onion, thinly sliced or
   chopped

1 teaspoon juniper berries,
   crushed (optional)
1 clove garlic, crushed
1 small carton natural
   yogurt
salt and pepper

This can be served with rice and VEGETABLES, CHINESE STYLE (p. 66), or a salad of watercress, lettuce and parsley.

METHOD

1   Cut the liver in very thin strips about 1½ inches long.
2   Melt the butter and oil over a low heat until foaming, add the onion, and juniper berries if using, together with the crushed garlic. Cook gently without browning for about 10 minutes.
3   Add the liver, increasing the heat to medium until evenly cooked. Be careful not to overcook.
4   When brown, turn the heat down, remove the pan from the heat and gently stir in the yogurt.
5   Return to the heat and gently simmer for 5 minutes. Season to taste.

Sicilian Pork/Veal

Serves 2
Cooking time: approximately 45 minutes

INGREDIENTS

⅓ chicken stock cube
1½ dessertspoons lemon
   juice
½ pint water
   (approximately)
1 teaspoon sugar
½ oz. margarine

½ onion, chopped
2 oz. mushrooms, sliced
8 oz. pork, trimmed and cut
   into 1-inch cubes
1 dessertspoon flour
¼ teaspoon dried herbs
salt and pepper

Serve with green vegetables.

METHOD

1 In a measuring jug, stir a third of a chicken stock cube
   into a quarter of a pint of boiling water. Add the lemon
   juice and make up to half a pint with hot or cold water.
   Stir in the teaspoon of sugar.
2 Melt the fat in a pan and sauté the onion until tender.
3 Add mushrooms and pork. Cook for 3–4 minutes.
4 Stir in the flour and remove from the heat. Gradually
   stir in the chicken stock mixture.
5 Add the herbs and season lightly with salt and pepper.
6 Bring to the boil and simmer for 40–45 minutes until
   the pork is tender. Adjust for seasoning.

Alternative: To make SICILIAN VEAL, substitute pie veal
for pork. *Or,* for a treat, use veal escalopes cut into large
strips, these only need simmering at step 6 for 10–15
minutes, until tender and cooked through.

Shrewsbury Lamb

Comment from Wolverhampton College of Adult Education Cookery Class: unusual ingredients, but rather tasty!

Serves 2
Oven temperature: 350°F, 180°C, gas mark 4
Cooking time: 1 hour if using the oven; or 30 minutes using the grill and top of the stove.

INGREDIENTS

2 lamb chops
1 oz. butter or margarine
4 oz. button mushrooms, sliced
1–2 tablespoons plain flour
½ pint of boiling stock
  mixed with

2 tablespoons redcurrant jelly
2 tablespoons Worcestershire sauce
juice of half a lemon
sprinkle of salt, pepper, grated nutmeg
chopped parsley to garnish

Serve with potatoes or bread and a green vegetable.

METHOD (oven cooking)

1   Fry the chops in the fat until brown on both sides. Remove to a casserole dish and cover with the sliced raw mushrooms.
2   Off the heat, stir 1 tablespoon of flour into the fat remaining in the pan, then gradually add the hot stock flavoured with the jelly, Worcestershire sauce, lemon and seasoning (you may need to fork the redcurrant jelly into the stock to help it to dissolve).

3   Return to the heat, bring to the boil, stirring continuously, and pour over the chops and mushrooms.
4   Cover the casserole dish and bake at 350°F, 180°C, gas mark 4 for 1 hour.
5   Sprinkle with parsley before serving.

ALTERNATIVE METHOD (using the grill and top of the stove)

1   Grill the seasoned chops till cooked through (approx. 20–25 minutes, depending on thickness).
2   Meanwhile, fry the mushrooms in the fat and stir in 2 tablespoons of flour for a minute or two. Then take off the heat and gradually add the stock mixture.
3   Return to the heat and simmer this well-flavoured mushroom sauce until the chops are ready. Pour the sauce over the grilled chops, sprinkle with parsley and serve.

Sweet and Sour Spare-ribs of Lamb

Serves 4: 2 servings hot one day, 2 servings cold the next day
Oven temperature: 325°F, 160°C, gas mark 3, reduce later to
300°F, 150°C, gas mark 2
Cooking time: approximately 70 minutes

INGREDIENTS

a whole unboned breast of
   lamb, meaty and of good
   quality
salt and pepper

1 tablespoon golden syrup
1 dessertspoon vinegar (malt
   or wine vinegar)

METHOD

1   Season the lamb and roast for 40 minutes at 325°F, 160°C, gas mark 3.
2   Remove to a dish so that you can pour off the fat from the tin.
3   Turn down the oven to 300°F, 150°C, gas mark 2.
4   Take two tablespoons of the fat poured off from the tin and put it in a saucepan with the golden syrup and vinegar. Bring to boil.
5   Return the lamb to the tin and pour over the sauce from the pan.
6   Return to the oven for half an hour or more, basting and turning.

Notes: A small scrubbed potato about 4-oz. size can be baked in its jacket at the same time.

   This sweet and sour recipe is also suitable for ribs of pork.

Saucer Pies

These individual pies do not need a special tin; they can be baked on old china saucers – the saucer will not break in the heat of the oven. Try savoury egg and bacon, or sweet fruit or jam saucer pies.

Egg and Bacon Saucer Pies

Serves 2
Oven temperature and cooking time: 400°F, 200°C, gas mark 6 for 15 minutes, reduce to 325°F, 160°C, gas mark 3 for the next 10–15 minutes

INGREDIENTS

Pastry
2½ oz. soft margarine
1 tablespoon water

4 oz. plain flour, sieved

Filling
4 rashers streaky bacon,
   chopped and fried in
   ½ oz. margarine (a
   small knob)
2 eggs, size 4, beaten

2 tablespoons milk
a pinch of pepper
a pinch of mixed herbs
   (optional)
milk to glaze

METHOD

To make pastry

1   Place the margarine, water and 2 tablespoons flour in a bowl and cream together with a fork until well mixed (half a minute).

2   Stir in the remaining flour to form a firm dough.
3   Knead lightly on a floured board. Divide in half. Roll out thinly to cut two rounds from each half, slightly larger than the saucer. Line the two saucers with the first two rounds of pastry and prick to prevent rising.

To make the filling and finish the pies

4   Combine all the ingredients and pour into the two saucers.
5   With a little water, damp round the edges of the pastry in the saucers. Cover the tops of the saucers with the third and fourth rounds and press on firmly. Brush with milk.
6   Place on a baking sheet and bake in a pre-heated hot oven at 400°F, 200°C, gas mark 6, for 15 minutes, then reduce heat to 325°F, 160°C, gas mark 3 for 10–15 minutes.

Note: If you prefer, this can be baked on a 6-inch pie plate or sandwich tin as one pie sufficient for 2–3 servings. For this one larger pie, bake at 400°F, 200°C, gas mark 6 for 25 minutes then reduce heat to 325°F, 160°C, gas mark 3 for the next 10–15 minutes.

For Sweet Saucer Pies

Make in the same way, but put in a filling of mincemeat and chopped apple, or canned gooseberries, plums or rhubarb. *Or* make uncovered pies, filled with jam or mincemeat. Uncovered pies cook in 15 minutes altogether.

Apple and Date Wholemeal Crumble

Serves 2, or 1 serving hot, 1 serving cold the next day
Oven temperature: 375°F, 190°C, gas mark 5
Cooking time: 25–30 minutes

INGREDIENTS

Crumble
¾ oz. margarine
1 oz. wholemeal flour
1 oz. porridge oats
½ oz. brown sugar
1 tablespoon oil

Filling
1 cooking apple, peeled,
   cored and chopped
a few chopped dates
1–2 tablespoons water
sugar to sweeten (optional)

Serve with cream, custard or natural yogurt.

METHOD

1 Make the crumble by rubbing margarine into flour and oats.
2 Stir in the sugar and oil.
3 Place the apples, dates, water and sugar in a baking dish.
4 Sprinkle the crumble over the fruit.
5 Bake 25–30 minutes, or until golden brown, 375°F, 190°C, gas mark 5.

Apple Parcel

As with all 'parcel' cooking, the taste of this is especially good. The full flavour is sealed in.

Serves 1 or 2
Oven temperature: 350°F, 180°C, gas mark 4
Cooking time: 25–30 minutes
You will need a piece of kitchen foil 12 inches square.

INGREDIENTS

a little butter
1 large cooking apple
a little lemon juice
1 rounded tablespoon
  sultanas

1 rounded dessertspoon soft
  brown sugar, or any
  available sugar
cream or top of the milk

METHOD

1 Butter the inner surface of the square of kitchen foil.
2 Peel and slice the apple and pile up on the buttered foil.
3 Sprinkle with the lemon juice, and stir in the sultanas and sugar.
4 Fold up the ends of the foil centrally to make a parcel and bake in centre of oven at 350°F, 180°C, gas mark 4, for 25–30 minutes.
5 Turn out on to a fruit dish and serve with cream or top of the milk.

Blackcurrant Jelly Creams

Serves 2, or make double quantities to serve again next day

INGREDIENTS

¼ pint of boiling water
half a packet blackcurrant
   jelly*

half a small can
   blackcurrants*
juice from the can
half a small can evaporated
   milk

* or use orange jelly, with mandarin oranges canned in fruit juice.

METHOD

1   Dissolve the jelly in the boiling water, and add the fruit juice. Allow to cool but not set.
2   Slowly pour the evaporated milk into the jelly, beating with a fork.
3   Stir in the fruit and chill until set.

Fresh Fruit Salad

Yes, I know it is easier to open a can of fruit cocktail, but once you have tasted the refreshing flavour of this fresh fruit salad you will know why I have purposely suggested enough for several servings. It looks and tastes just as good next day. If you are visiting invalid or tired elderly friends, this is a treat you could prepare for them.

Serves 3–4

INGREDIENTS

3 level tablespoons
  granulated sugar
1 teacup water
juice of 1 lemon

fruit, e.g., 1 orange, 1 apple,
  1 banana, 1 pear, other
  fresh fruit in season

METHOD

1 Bring the sugar and water to the boil, while stirring, then simmer without stirring it for approximately 5 minutes. Allow to cool.
2 Stir in the lemon juice.
3 Meanwhile peel and cut up the fruit and put it in a bowl. Pour the cold syrup over the fruit and leave for at least half an hour before serving.

Note: The 'ordinary' fruits were the most popular with the classes, with the addition of a few grapes, or soft fruits in season.

Orange Semolina Jelly

Serves 2–3
An easily digested, nourishing jelly

INGREDIENTS

half a packet orange jelly
¼ pint of boiling water
1 tablespoon orange juice
½ pint of milk

½ oz. margarine or butter
2 level tablespoons semolina
2 level tablespoons sugar

METHOD

1   Dissolve the jelly in the boiling water, leave to cool but not set. Add the orange juice.
2   Heat the milk and margarine, sprinkle on the semolina and bring to the boil, stirring. Continue to simmer gently for 10 minutes, stirring all the time as it thickens and cooks. Stir in the sugar and allow to cool.
3   Stir the cooled jelly into the cooled semolina, mixing well. It can be poured into individual dishes or left in a large bowl. Leave to set.

Store-cupboard alternative: Stir the cooled jelly and orange juice into canned semolina pudding.

Lemon Sponge Pudding

Comment from Harlow Technical College Classes: 'The sponge rises, leaving a thick lemony sauce beneath. All liked this recipe very much and were very surprised how delicious the result was. Do use the soft easy-creaming margarine, it is so much easier to whisk than harder ones.'

Serves 2–3
Oven temperature: 350°F, 180°C, gas mark 4
Cooking time: 20–30 minutes
You will need a medium-sized pie dish (of about three quarters of a pint capacity)

INGREDIENTS

juice and rind of half a
　lemon
1 oz. soft, easy-creaming
　margarine
2 oz. caster sugar

1 egg, size 3, separated
1 oz. self-raising flour,
　sieved
¼ pint (8 tablespoons) of
　water

Serve warm, sprinkled with caster sugar.

METHOD

1　Weigh and prepare all ingredients, placing all but the egg white in a mixing bowl.
2　Whisk egg white fairly stiffly in another bowl.
3　Whisk all ingredients (except egg white) in the mixing bowl until smooth (2–3 minutes). The mixture will seem very runny.

4   Fold in the beaten egg white carefully, using a metal
    spoon. Pour into a greased three-quarter-pint pie dish.
5   Bake in pre-heated moderate oven, 350°F, 180°C, gas
    mark 4 on middle shelf for 20–30 minutes.

Puffed Sweet Omelette

Something to celebrate? Or just feel you need a treat? Try this quick-to-make luxury omelette, recommended by the Swinton Adult Education Centre 'Cookery for Men' class.

Serves 1
You will need a small frying pan or omelette pan

INGREDIENTS

Omelette
2 eggs, size 3 or 4, separated
1 oz. caster sugar
a knob of butter
icing sugar

Filling
1 tablespoon warmed jam
or
2–3 oz. fresh strawberries,
    chopped and mixed with 1
    tablespoon sugar

METHOD

1   In one bowl, whisk the egg whites until they stand in soft peaks; whisk the yolks and caster sugar until they are creamy in another bowl. Fold the whites into the yolk mixture.
2   Melt the butter over moderate heat, pour in the omelette mixture and cook, without stirring, for 2 or 3 minutes until golden on the underside. Meanwhile, pre-heat the grill.

3   Place under a moderate grill for about 2 minutes, until
    the top is puffed and golden brown.
4   Make a mark with a knife or spatula at right angles to
    the pan handle, spread the filling over one side and fold
    the omelette over firmly.
5   Slide the omelette gently on to a warmed plate. Dust
    with a little sieved icing sugar before serving.

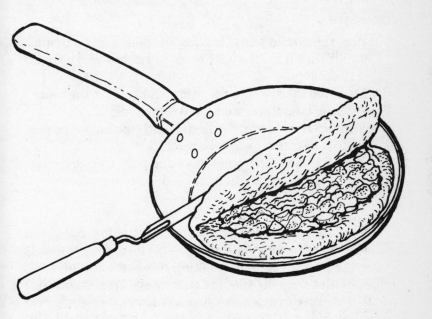

Poached Pears

Serves 2

INGREDIENTS

4 small, or 2 medium, firm
  dessert pears
4 tablespoons granulated
  sugar

¼ pint of water
2 cinnamon sticks
1 teaspoon lemon juice

METHOD

1 Peel the whole pears, leaving the stalks and cutting a
   small slice from the base to make them stand upright,
   if necessary.
2 Dissolve the sugar in the water and boil for 1 minute.
3 Add the cinnamon sticks and lemon juice.
4 Simmer the pears in the liquid, with the lid on the pan,
   for 20–30 minutes, until tender.
5 Remove the cinnamon sticks and pour the syrup over
   the pears. Serve warm or chilled.

Notes: The syrup thickens during the cooking, but if you
find it too runny just boil it down further before pouring
over the pears. I enjoyed cooking this – the kitchen was
filled with a fragrant smell of cinnamon. This is also good
with two or three whole cloves studded into each pear
before cooking.

Swedish Apple

Serves 2

INGREDIENTS

8 oz. cooking apples
approx. 2–3 tablespoons
 water
sugar to taste
1 small carton whipping
 cream

a small knob of butter or
 margarine
2 oz. fresh brown or white
 breadcrumbs
1 oz. demerara sugar

METHOD

1 Peel, core and quarter the apples. Stew with the water
   in a covered pan until they form a pulp. For some
   varieties of apple it may be necessary to stir once or
   twice and add a little more water.
2 Add sugar to taste. Cool and put into individual serving dishes.
3 Melt the butter or margarine and lightly fry the
   crumbs (or heat ready-made BUTTERED CRUMBS
   p. 246). Stir in the demerara sugar and leave to cool
   and crisp.
4 Whip the cream and spread on top of the apple in
   serving dishes. Sprinkle the breadcrumb and sugar
   mixture generously on top.

A speedy alternative: use freshly mashed banana in place
of the stewed apple.

Anzac Biscuits

These are similar to the popular BUTTON BISCUITS (page 197), but the tutor at Hounslow Borough College tells me that her students like the crunch of the coconut and find the rubbing-in method easy.

Makes approximately 30 small biscuits (they keep well in a tin or can be frozen).
Oven temperature: 325°F, 160°C, gas mark 3
Cooking time: 20 minutes

INGREDIENTS

2 oz. caster sugar
2 oz. plain flour
a pinch of salt
2 oz. desiccated coconut
2 oz. rolled oats
1½ oz. hard margarine

1½ oz. lard
¼ teaspoon bicarbonate of soda, *dissolved in* 1½ tablespoons milk

METHOD

1   Rub the fats into the dry ingredients.
2   Add the bicarbonate of soda and milk to bind to a firm dough, adding a little more milk if necessary.
3   Roll into sausages the diameter of a 10p piece and cut into thin slices, to make about 30 biscuits.
4   Place on a greased baking sheet and bake until *pale* golden brown at 325°F, 160°C, gas mark 3 for approximately 20 minutes.

Button Biscuits

Note from Camden Cookery Classes: the addition of a teaspoon of ground ginger with the flour makes these into delicious gingernuts.

Makes approximately 30 small biscuits (they keep well in a tin or can be frozen).
Oven temperature: 375°F, 190°C, gas mark 5
Cooking time: 8–10 minutes

INGREDIENTS

3 oz. self-raising flour,
   sieved
a pinch of salt
3 oz. caster sugar
3 oz. rolled oats

3 oz. butter or margarine
1 level tablespoon golden
   syrup
½ level teaspoon
   bicarbonate of soda
1 tablespoon milk

METHOD

1 Mix together the flour, salt, sugar and oats.
2 Warm the butter or margarine and syrup together until the fat has melted. Stir into the dry ingredients.
3 Dissolve the bicarbonate of soda in the milk and add to the mixture. Mix well.
4 Form the mixture into *small* balls, the size of marbles. Place on a greased baking tray, well apart.
5 Bake in a pre-heated oven 375°F, 190°C, gas mark 5, for 8–10 minutes until golden brown.
6 Cool for a few minutes on the baking tray, remove and cool on a wire rack. Store in an airtight tin.

Chocolate Marmalade Cake

Oven temperature: 350°F, 180°C, gas mark 4
Cooking time: 30–40 minutes

INGREDIENTS*

4 oz. soft margarine
4 oz. sugar (caster or soft brown)
4 oz. wholemeal flour
2 teaspoons baking powder
1½ tablespoons marmalade
2 eggs

1 level tablespoon cocoa
   plus
1 tablespoon boiling water to form a paste
a little water or milk if needed

METHOD

1   Grease and base-line a small loaf tin or a 6–7-inch sponge tin.
2   Put all ingredients into a bowl and mix to a soft consistency, adding a little water or milk if necessary.
3   Spoon into the prepared tin and bake at 350°F, 180°C, gas mark 4 for 30–40 minutes.

* Half quantities can be made, and baked in a 5-inch tin.

Chocolate Muesli Bars

Note from Wythenshawe class: 'This we found very rich, but very moreish!' You only need a small portion.

Makes 16 small squares (no baking)
You will need a 7-inch square shallow tin, greased and base-lined

INGREDIENTS

1¾ oz. butter or margarine
1 tablespoon golden syrup
4 oz. muesli

1 oz. sultanas or seedless raisins
1 oz. glacé cherries, chopped
3–4 oz. plain chocolate

METHOD

1   Melt the fat in a saucepan and add the syrup.
2   Remove from the heat and stir in the muesli, raisins and cherries.
3   Press into the greased and lined shallow tin.
4   Melt the chocolate in a basin over hot water and spread over the mixture in the tin. Chill in the refrigerator for half an hour or until set.
5   Cut into squares or fingers.

Note from test-cooking: You also need a finger bowl, flannel or finger-licking as you eat! Delicious . . .

Coconut Slices

Note from Swinton Adult Education Centre 'Cookery for Men' class: Make sure it is cooled completely at step 5, otherwise the chocolate may peel away with the paper.

These coconut slices were thoroughly enjoyed by all in the class. Had they left any they would have kept for several days in an airtight tin.

Makes 16 narrow slices
Oven temperature: 350°F, 180°C, gas mark 4
Cooking time: 20–25 minutes
You will need a 7-inch square shallow tin (non-stick or lightly greased around the sides), base-lined with baking parchment.

INGREDIENTS

2 oz. plain chocolate
3 oz. caster sugar
1½ oz. soft margarine

1 egg, size 4
3 oz. desiccated coconut

METHOD

1　Melt chocolate in a basin over hot water. Spread it evenly over the paper in the tin. Leave to cool and set.
2　Cream sugar and margarine until soft and fluffy.
3　Beat in the egg and coconut.
4　Spread over the set chocolate and bake at 350°F, 180°C, gas mark 4 until golden, about 20–25 minutes.
5　Leave to get completely cold before turning out and peeling off the paper.
6　Cut across in half, then cut each half down into eight strips to make slices approximately 3 × 1 inch.

Crumble Shortbread

This is easier than the normal kneading method.

Oven temperature: 325–350°F, 160–180°C, gas mark 3–4
Cooking time: 30 minutes

INGREDIENTS

4 oz. plain flour
2 oz. cornflour, rice flour or custard powder*

4 oz. butter
2 oz. caster sugar, plus a little for sprinkling later

* We have put custard powder as an alternative ingredient in this recipe as you may have it in the store-cupboard. But use cornflour or rice flour in preference – they give a better result in this recipe.

METHOD

1 Grease a sandwich tin.
2 Measure all the ingredients into a bowl and rub in the butter until mixture is crumbly.
3 Put spoonfuls into the greased sandwich tin taking care to press down very gently. If pressed too hard the shortbread will be hard and tough.
4 Bake in a moderate oven (325–350°F, 160–180°C, gas mark 3–4) for about 30 minutes. The shortbread will be pale golden and firm to the touch when cooked – but be careful when touching it: it is hot.
5 Sprinkle a little more caster sugar over the top while it is still hot, and leave to cool in the tin.
6 Divide the shortbread into sections while it is still in the tin – though the traditional way to serve is to break off portions.

Eggless Chocolate Cake

Comment from Sheffield cookery classes: 'This was thought to be a very good recipe. They were surprised that an eggless cake recipe could turn out so well.'

Oven temperature: 350°F, 180°C, gas mark 4
Cooking time: 20–25 minutes
You will need two 6-inch sandwich tins, or one 8-inch sandwich tin

INGREDIENTS

4 oz. plain flour
4 oz. caster sugar
2 rounded tablespoons cocoa
large pinch bicarbonate of soda
½ level teaspoon baking powder
¼ level teaspoon salt
4 fl. oz. milk
½ teaspoon vinegar
2 fl. oz. corn oil
few drops vanilla essence

METHOD

1 Grease and line the base of two 6-inch sandwich tins or one 8-inch sandwich tin with greased greaseproof paper or ungreased baking parchment.
2 Sieve all the dry ingredients together into a mixing bowl.
3 Whisk together the milk, vinegar, corn oil and vanilla essence with a fork, and add to the dry ingredients. Beat well with a wooden spoon to form a smooth slack mixture. Turn into prepared tins.
4 Bake in a moderate oven 350°F, 180°C, gas mark 4 for about 20 minutes (an 8-inch tin requires 25 minutes).

The cake should be firm to the touch and have just shrunk away from the side of the tin.

5 Cool on a cake tray, remove paper carefully.

6 To decorate the single 8-inch cake, sieve a little icing sugar over the top. To sandwich together the two 6-inch cakes, use One-stage Icing or Filling (page 204) preferably making the chocolate or coffee variation.

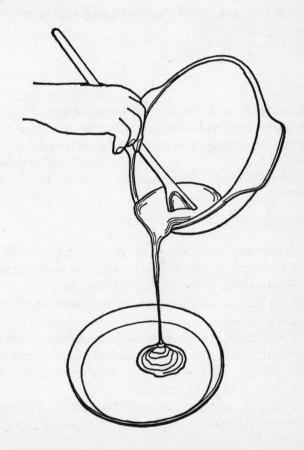

'One-stage' Icing or Filling

INGREDIENTS

1½ oz. soft margarine
4 oz. icing sugar, sieved

1 dessertspoon milk or fruit
  juice

METHOD

Place all ingredients in mixing bowl and beat until well mixed (2–3 minutes).

Variations

Chocolate: blend 1 dessertspoon cocoa with 1 tablespoon hot water, cool and add to basic recipe instead of the milk.
Orange or lemon: use fruit juice instead of milk. Add colouring.
Coffee: replace 1 dessertspoon milk by 1 dessertspoon Camp Coffee Essence.

Everyday Fruit Cake

Oven temperature: 350°F, 180°C, gas mark 4
Cooking time: 45 minutes to 1 hour
You will need a 1-lb. loaf tin

INGREDIENTS

4 oz. self-raising flour
2 oz. margarine
3 oz. mixed dried fruit
2½ oz. caster sugar

1 egg, size 4
2½ tablespoons milk

METHOD

1   Grease or line the loaf tin.
2   Sieve the flour into a mixing bowl and rub in the margarine.
3   Add the fruit and sugar and mix well.
4   Beat the egg with the milk and stir sufficient into the dry ingredients to make a dropping consistency.*
5   Turn into the prepared tin and bake at 350°F, 180°C, gas mark 4.
6   Turn out and cool on a wire tray.

Notes: Add the egg and milk gradually. If a larger egg is used, it could make the mixture too soft. The cake will be cooked when the surface feels firm and has begun to shrink slightly from the sides of the tin.

*   Lift up a spoonful of the mixture and hold it steadily against the side of the mixing bowl. The lump should drop easily from the spoon within a few seconds.

Milk Chocolate Cake

This sticky chocolate cake is a favourite with the Richmond 'Cookery for the Visually Disabled' class.

Oven temperature: 325°F, 160°C, gas mark 3
Cooking time: approximately 35 minutes
You will need two 7–8-inch sponge tins, greased and base-lined

INGREDIENTS

Cake
7 oz. self-raising flour
a pinch of salt
8 oz. caster sugar
2 tablespoons cocoa
4 oz. margarine
2 eggs beaten with 5
    tablespoons water *and*
5 tablespoons evaporated
    milk
1 teaspoon vanilla essence

Filling
1½ oz. margarine
4 oz. icing sugar
2 tablespoons milk
1 tablespoon cocoa
½ teaspoon vanilla essence

METHOD

1 Sift together the flour, salt, sugar and cocoa.
2 Rub in the margarine.

3 Stir in the eggs, liquids and vanilla essence and beat well. It will be runny.

4 Pour into the prepared tins.

5 Bake on the middle shelf at 325°F, 160°C, gas mark 3 for about 35 minutes, until risen, just firm to the touch and beginning to come away from the sides of the tin.

6 For the filling, place all the ingredients in a bowl over a pan of hot water. Stir until smooth and glossy, then beat, using a beater or an electric whisk to combine the ingredients so that they thicken as they cool. Spread over one cake and sandwich the second cake on top.

Mincemeat Cake, Plus

The 'plus' can be either 3 or 4 buns or 2 individual puddings, taken from the mixture and cooked for yourself. Then the cake (which is a light, plain fruit cake) can be served separately for a tea party.

Oven temperature: 375°F, 190°C, gas mark 5, reduced after 15 minutes to 325°F, 160°C, gas mark 3
Cooking time: approx. 70 minutes for the cake, approx. 20 minutes for the buns/puddings
You will need a patty tin and paper cases or small individual foil pie dishes, plus a 1-lb. loaf tin or a 7–8-inch deep loose-bottom cake tin (non-stick or greased and base-lined)

INGREDIENTS (see Yogurt Pot Measures, page 249)

4 oz. (1 pot) soft brown sugar	8 oz. (1 pot) mincemeat
7 oz. (2 pots) self-raising flour	4 oz. soft margarine
	2 eggs, size 2, unbeaten

METHOD

1   In a bowl, beat all the ingredients together well for a minute or two.
2   Transfer 4 tablespoons of the mixture into 3 or 4 paper cases in patty tins or into 2 greased individual foil pie dishes. Transfer the rest of the mixture to the cake tin.
3   Bake the cake and buns or puddings at 375°F, 190°C, gas mark 5 for 15 minutes.
4   Reduce the heat, and continue baking at 325°F, 160°C, gas mark 3.

5   Test the buns/puddings after 15–20 minutes, and the cake after 1 hour (they should be just firm to the touch). Continue cooking for a few more minutes if necessary.

Note: The little puddings can be served hot with custard; the cake and buns should be cooled on a wire rack. They keep well for several days in an airtight tin.

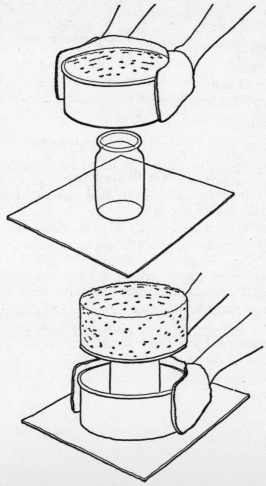

Iced Buns

Makes 9 or 10
Oven temperature: 375°F, 190°C, gas mark 5
Cooking time: 15–20 minutes

INGREDIENTS

Buns
4 oz. self-raising flour,
   sieved
2 oz. margarine
2 oz. caster sugar
1 egg, size 1, beaten
1½ tablespoons marmalade
dash of milk if necessary

Icing
4 oz. icing sugar, sieved
2 tablespoons lemon juice

METHOD

1   Line 9 or 10 patty tins with paper cases.
2   Cream margarine and sugar until light and fluffy and gradually beat in the egg.
3   Stir in the marmalade and fold in the flour with a little milk if necessary to give a dropping consistency.* Half fill the paper cases.
4   Bake at 375°F, 190°C, gas mark 5 for 15–20 minutes. Cool on a wire tray.
5   Mix the icing sugar with sufficient lemon juice to make a soft spread. Top each bun with this lemon glacé icing.

* See page 205

No-Bake Chocolate Rum Cake

In every book that concentrates on nourishment and economy, I think there should be one wicked and extravagant recipe: this is it!

Makes 8 small portions and can be kept for several days in a refrigerator
You will need a 1-lb. loaf tin or a 1-pint dish, base-lined with baking parchment or greaseproof paper

INGREDIENTS

4 oz. butter
4 oz. plain cooking
   chocolate
2 oz. glacé cherries, chopped
2 oz. chopped nuts (walnuts, almonds, hazelnuts)*

4 oz. plain sweet biscuits
1 egg, size 4
1½ oz. caster sugar
1 tablespoon rum (or brandy)

* These can be bought ready-chopped.

METHOD

1   Gently melt the butter and chocolate together (this can be done over a pan of hot water). Cool slightly.
2   Break the biscuits into small pieces and mix with the chopped cherries and nuts.
3   Whisk the egg and sugar until pale and thick. Fold in the chocolate mixture with the rum or brandy. Then stir in the biscuits, cherries and nuts.
4   Pour into the tin or dish and leave to set in a cool place, preferably a refrigerator. Cut into deliciously sticky slices and serve.

Wholemeal Date Shortbread

Oven temperature: 325°F, 160°C, gas mark 3
Cooking time: approximately 40 minutes

INGREDIENTS

4 oz. stoned chopped dates*
1 lemon – grated rind and juice
4 oz. butter or margarine
2 oz. soft brown sugar
5 oz. wholemeal or 81% flour } or 6 oz. wholewheat flour
1 oz. cornflour, or rice flour
1 teaspoon baking powder

* Can be bought ready-chopped in packets

METHOD

1   Put the dates, lemon rind and juice into a pan and cook until soft and mushy. Add a little water if necessary.
2   Allow to cool.
3   In a mixing bowl, cream together the fat and sugar.
4   Sieve together the flour, baking powder and cornflour. Add to the creamed mixture to form a stiff dough.
5   Divide into two parts. Press one part into a greased 7-inch tin or flan ring.
6   Spread the date mixture over this shortbread, leaving a border of a quarter of an inch. Roll out the rest of the mixture on greaseproof paper, lift on to the dates to make a sandwich, and press the edges together.
7   Prick the surface with a fork.
8   Bake at 325°F, 160°C, gas mark 3 for 40 minutes or until golden.

Variations

Instead of the dates you could use:
mixed dried fruit; *or*
a mixture of apple, and mixed dried fruit or dried apricots.
    You could also sprinkle the shortbread with nuts before
baking.

Chapter 5

Store-cupboard Cookery

Contents

Bad weather or temporary illness can keep even the most enthusiastic shoppers indoors. Many other men and women are permanently housebound and for them shopping is often a matter of relying on others to bring in their food.

Under these conditions it is all too easy to find yourself living on dull and boring snacks and limiting your enjoyment of meal times.

This chapter has been written to help you with your difficulties. As well as the usual background stocks of milk, cheese, eggs, fats and regularly used dried goods, if you have the following items in stock you will be able to make, without need of shopping, all the recipes in this chapter. Look through the other chapters too: the goods listed below will enable you to cook many of the other recipes from your stores.

Shopping Check-list for Your Emergency Food Store-cupboard

Choose from this check-list the items of greatest value for you and see that you always have them in stock. Ideally, choose a few items from each heading. Keep a regular turn-over, because foods do not last for ever.

Beverages

Favourite milk drink, e.g., cocoa, Horlicks, Ovaltine
Tea, coffee
Soups, including condensed
Build Up or Complan – choice of natural, savoury or sweet
    flavours

Vitamin C Drinks

Long-life carton fruit juices, e.g., orange, grapefruit,
   blackcurrant (or bottled vitamin C blackcurrant cordial)
Canned juices, e.g., orange, grapefruit, tomato

Note: Some fruit squashes do not contain vitamin C –
check the label.

Milk and Milk Products

Condensed or evaporated milk
Long-life milk, milk powder
Canned milk puddings

Cereals

Porridge oats, or other breakfast cereals, including high-fibre
   cereals, e.g., bran flakes, muesli
Flour, rice
Semolina, or other pudding cereals
Macaroni, spaghetti or other pasta

Meat (canned)

Chicken
Corned beef
Ham
Frankfurters

Liver paté
Luncheon meat
Minced meat
Stewed steak

Fish (canned)

Fish roes   Pilchards
Fish spreads   Sardines or sild
Kippers   Tuna or salmon
Mackerel

Fats

Butter, margarine, cooking fat
Cooking oil

Fruit and Vegetables

Canned fruits, including one-portion cans
Canned vegetables, including canned tomatoes
Instant potatoes (check label for vitamin C)
Canned beans and garden peas
Dried peas, beans and lentils, dried onions
Dried fruit, e.g., prunes, sultanas

Note: Frozen fruits and vegetables generally retain their vitamin C value. The heat of canning destroys some vitamin C. Dried foods generally do not provide the vitamin unless the manufacturer has added it.

Other Groceries

Yeast extract/Marmite
Meat extract, stock cubes

Packet sauces
Sugar
Marmalade, jam, golden syrup, honey
Biscuits (sweet and savoury), crispbread
Jellies, packet desserts, custard powder

Flavourings

Salt, pepper, mustard, curry powder or paste, vinegar
Herbs and spices
Pickles and chutneys
Tomato purée and ketchup, Worcestershire sauce
Vanilla, almond and other essences, lemon juice

Frozen Foods

If you have a freezer you can stock a variety of ready-bought or
home-cooked frozen foods in one or two portions.
Basic freezer stocks can include sliced bread, prepared
breadcrumbs, grated cheese, vegetable purées for soups,
whole sliced lemons, frozen orange juice, cooked tartlet
cases, uncooked prepared pastry or biscuit mix, slices of
cake, ice cubes.

As well as the emergency food store, you need fresh
foods bought more frequently, such as fruit, vegetables,
milk, cheeses, yogurt, bread, eggs, bacon, meat, poultry
and fish.

Soup Scramble

Serves 2
For one person use 2 size 4 eggs to the one small can of soup
Cooking time: 3 or 4 minutes

INGREDIENTS

3 eggs, size 3 or 4   2 rounds of buttered toast
1 small 5-oz. can condensed
    soup (celery, asparagus,
    mushroom or chicken are
    all equally suitable)

METHOD

1   Turn out the undiluted soup into a saucepan.
2   Add the eggs and beat vigorously into the soup with a
    fork.
3   Stir continuously with a spoon over moderate heat
    until the eggs absorb the soup and become a thick,
    well-flavoured scrambled egg.
4   Serve at once on rounds of buttered toast.

Savoury Soufflé

This is more expensive than the simple one-stage cheese soufflé, but may be a more convenient alternative, if you already have a packet of sauce-mix, or a small can of condensed soup in your cupboard.

Serves 2

Note: For a single serving make up half the recipe and cook in a 3-inch-diameter soufflé dish.

Oven temperature: 375°F, 190°C, gas mark 5
Cooking time: approximately 25 minutes (15–20 minutes for single serving)

INGREDIENTS

either	*or*
1 packet sauce-mix (e.g., cheese flavour)	a 5-oz. can of condensed soup (e.g., mushroom, chicken or celery)
and	
¼ pint of milk (8 tablespoons)	2 eggs, size 3 or 4, separated

METHOD

1　Grease a 5-inch-diameter ovenproof dish, preferably a soufflé dish.
2　*If using sauce-mix*
In a medium-sized saucepan (*and using only quarter of a pint of milk*) make up the sauce by the method given

on the packet. Remove this thick sauce from the heat and allow to cool for a minute or two.

If using condensed soup

In a medium-sized saucepan, stir the undiluted contents of the can until smooth and hot, then remove this thick 'sauce' from the heat and allow to cool for a minute or two.

3 Stir in the egg yolks.

4 Whisk the egg whites stiffly, then with a large metal spoon, gently cut and fold the egg whites into the contents of the saucepan.

5 Pour into the dish and bake in a fairly hot oven, 375°F, 190°C, gas mark 5 for approximately 25 minutes (approximately 15–20 minutes for a single serving) till well risen and golden.

6 Serve at once.

Curried Mayonnaise

INGREDIENTS

6 tablespoons mayonnaise
(home-made, or its nearest
shop-bought equivalent)

¾ teaspoon mild curry paste
1 dessert apple (optional)

Serve with hard-boiled eggs
        or cold, cut up chicken   } on a bed of salad
        or cold steamed or grilled fish

METHOD

1   Place the curry paste in a small bowl and gradually mix
     in the mayonnaise until thoroughly blended.
2   If liked, grate in a little dessert apple.

Herring Roes on Toast

Serves 1

INGREDIENTS

4–5 oz. (125 g) soft herring
  roes (fresh or – for a
  store-cupboard recipe –
  canned roes)
approximately 1 level   .
  tablespoon plain flour

salt and pepper
1 oz. butter or margarine
1 slice of bread
butter and Marmite for
  spreading

METHOD

1   Season the flour with salt and pepper and toss the roes
    in it (easily done if you shake them all together in a
    clean paper bag).
2   Melt the butter in a small frying-pan, and fry the roes
    for 4–5 minutes, turning them in the pan until they are
    lightly browned.
3   Toast the bread. Spread with butter and Marmite.
4   Place the roes on the Marmite toast, and pour over
    them any butter still in the pan.
5   Serve piping hot.

Savoury Spreads

Digestible Sardine

INGREDIENTS

1 can sardines
1 small egg

METHOD

1   Drain the sardines from the oil, and mash.
2   Beat the egg and gradually add to the mashed sardines
    to make a smooth mixture. Serve on hot toast.

Note: Sardines mixed like this with raw beaten egg seem
to be more digestible. This pleasant spread could also be
served with salad.

Liver-sausage and Egg

INGREDIENTS

1 egg   2 oz. liver-sausage, *or* a
                                             small tin of pâté

METHOD

1   Hard boil the egg, cool and chop.
2   Mix with the liver-sausage.

Tuna and Tomato

INGREDIENTS

1 small can tuna fish or pink
   salmon

3 tablespoons tomato
   ketchup

METHOD

1   Flake the fish with a fork.
2   Blend well with the tomato ketchup.

Sweet Spreads

Chocolate Spread

INGREDIENTS

2 oz. soft, easy-creaming
  margarine
2 tablespoons cocoa powder
½ tablespoon black
  treacle

1 tablespoon condensed
  milk
vanilla essence, or grated
  orange rind

Serve on fruit bread, malt bread or buns, or use as a cake filling.

METHOD

1   Mix the margarine, cocoa powder, treacle and condensed milk well together.
2   Add grated orange rind or one or two drops of vanilla essence to flavour.

Note: This spread keeps for a month in a screw-topped jar or sealed plastic container in a cold larder or refrigerator.

Goulash

Serves 2, or one serving one day and, thoroughly reheated, a second serving next day.
Cooking time: 15 minutes

INGREDIENTS

a knob of margarine or
   dripping
1 level tablespoon plain
   flour
1 tablespoon dried onion
a 7½-oz. can stewed steak

1 tablespoon tomato purée
1 level teaspoon paprika
a scant ¼ pint of stock (¼
   beef stock cube dissolved
   in ¼ pint of water)
seasoning

Serve on a bed of mashed potato, or plain boiled rice.

METHOD

1 Melt the fat in a saucepan.
2 Add the flour, onion, stewed steak, tomato purée and paprika and cook for 2–3 minutes, stirring continuously.
3 Add stock, season to taste, simmer gently with the lid on the pan for 10–12 minutes.

Ham and Vegetable Rice

Serves 2
Cooking time: approximately 25–30 minutes

INGREDIENTS

4 oz. cooked ham or
  luncheon meat, diced*
2 tablespoons cooked peas,
  or 5-oz. can garden peas
2 oz. chopped onion, or 1
  heaped teaspoon dried
  onion

an 8-oz. (227 g.) can peeled
  tomatoes with the juice
salt and pepper to taste
¼ pint of stock
2 oz. uncooked long-grain
  rice

* Cheaper alternative, suggested by Bedale Agricultural
Centre Retirement Class: 'Use bacon pieces, first fried then
added to ingredients, in place of ham or luncheon meat.' This,
of course, takes it out of the 'store-cupboard cookery' chapter,
but is well worth trying.

METHOD

1 Combine all ingredients except rice in a saucepan and
  bring to the boil. Simmer for 10 minutes.
2 Stir in the rice. Bring back to the boil and stir once,
  lower the heat and simmer. Cover the pan and cook for
  about 15 minutes, or until the rice is soft and the liquid
  is absorbed.

Spaghetti Bolognese

Serves 2
Cooking time: 20 minutes

INGREDIENTS

a 7½-oz. can of minced beef
2 tablespoons minestrone
  soup mix

¼ pint of water
3 oz. spaghetti

Serving suggestion: sprinkle with Parmesan cheese.

METHOD

1 Place the minced beef in a saucepan and stir in the dry
   soup powder and add the water.
2 Bring to the boil and allow to simmer for 20 minutes.
3 Meanwhile, in a medium-size saucepan, bring some
   salted water to the boil, add the spaghetti, keep the lid
   off and boil fast until the spaghetti is just soft, about 10
   minutes. Drain.
4 Serve the meat sauce poured over the spaghetti.

Note: For those who find spaghetti difficult to manage: try
the easy-to-eat pasta shapes, e.g., shells or spirals.

Baked Custard

Serves 2
The addition of the milk powder gives extra nourishment and creaminess.
Oven temperature: 300°F, 150°C, gas mark 2
Cooking time: 1 hour

INGREDIENTS

1 egg, size 3 or 4
1½ level tablespoons
   skimmed milk powder

1 level tablespoon
   granulated sugar
½ pint of milk
grated nutmeg (optional)

METHOD

1   Beat the egg, skimmed milk powder and sugar together.
2   Heat the milk, but do not boil, and pour onto the egg mixture. Strain into an ovenproof dish. Sprinkle with a little nutmeg if liked.
3   Bake in a slow oven 300°F, 150°C, gas mark 2, until the custard is set, about 1 hour.

Bread Pudding

Serves 2
Oven temperature: 350°F, 180°C, gas mark 4
Cooking time: 1 hour 15 minutes

INGREDIENTS

4 oz. stale brown or white
  bread (crusts left on)
3 tablespoons mixed dried
  fruit
1 tablespoon chopped peel

1 tablespoon shredded suet
or melted margarine
¼ teaspoon ground mixed
  spice
2 dessertspoons golden
  syrup

METHOD

1 Soak the bread in water until just softened. Press in a
   sieve until it is as dry as possible.
2 Transfer to a bowl and beat with a fork to get rid of any
   lumps. Add the rest of the ingredients and mix well.
3 Turn the mixture into a small greased ovenproof dish
   and bake at 350°F, 180°C, gas mark 4 for about an hour
   and a quarter, until crisp and brown on top.
4 Sprinkle with granulated sugar and serve hot or cold.

Chocolate Mousse

Serves 1, but quantities can be multiplied for more servings

INGREDIENTS

1 oz. plain chocolate
1 teaspoon milk or water

1 egg, separated

METHOD

1   Melt the chocolate slowly with the milk or water in a basin over a pan of hot (not boiling) water, stirring to blend.
2   Remove from the heat and beat in the egg yolk.
3   Whisk the egg white until stiff and carefully fold into the chocolate mixture.
4   Pour into a small dish and leave to cool.

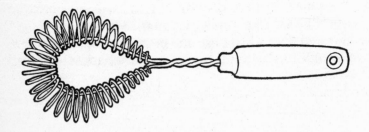

Fruit in Batter (Clafoutis)

Serves 2
Oven temperature: 400°F, 200°C, gas mark 6
Cooking time: approximately 45 minutes

INGREDIENTS

a knob of butter
1 egg, size 1
1 oz. caster sugar
1½ oz. flour
¼ pint of milk

1 small can apricots, drained
    from the juice
or 4 oz. fresh fruit, e.g.,
    raspberries or stoned
    cherries
caster sugar for sprinkling

METHOD

1 Grease a shallow ovenproof dish (the size of a soup plate).
2 Whisk the egg and sugar until pale and thick. Fold in the flour and then stir in the milk.
3 Pour half of this batter into the dish and bake at 400°F, 200°C, gas mark 6 for 15 minutes.
4 Arrange the fruit on top and pour on remaining batter. Return to the oven for a further 30 minutes, until golden.
5 Sprinkle with caster sugar before serving.

Hot Chocolate Rice

Serves 1

INGREDIENTS

1 small can creamed rice
  pudding, or some
  home-made rice pudding

1 tablespoon drinking
  chocolate

METHOD

1   Turn out the rice pudding into a small saucepan.
2   Stir in the chocolate powder.
3   Heat gently, stirring.

Note: Try this served with sliced raw banana.

Orange Rice

Serves 1

INGREDIENTS

1 small can creamed rice
 pudding, or some
 home-made rice pudding

1 tablespoon frozen orange
 juice, thawed and
 undiluted

METHOD

1   Empty the rice into a bowl and stir in the thawed
    undiluted orange juice.
2   Serve cold or chilled.

Note: Use the rest of the juice, diluted, for refreshing
drinks (try it for PEPTAIL (page 45) for the next day's
breakfast).

Raspberry Honeycomb

Serves 2–3

INGREDIENTS

1 small can raspberries
half a packet raspberry jelly

1 egg, separated

METHOD

1 Strain the fruit and set aside.
2 To the juice add sufficient water to make 8 oz. (If you have no fluid ounces marked on a measure, reckon 8 oz. to equal 1 small teacup.) Heat the liquid and dissolve the jelly in it. Allow to cool for approximately 3 minutes.
3 Beat the egg yolk into the slightly cooled liquid. Add the fruit.
4 Whisk the egg white until fairly stiff, cut and fold into the mixture with a metal spoon.
5 Pour into serving dish, or individual glasses, and leave to set. The mixture will separate with a thick fruit jelly underneath and a frothy pink layer on top.

Variations: Add a little lemon juice to sharpen the flavour and use mandarin oranges, blackcurrants or gooseberries to ring the changes.

Soufflé Ground Rice

Serves 2

INGREDIENTS

1 tablespoon ground rice
1 tablespoon sugar
1 tablespoon cocoa
  (optional)

½ pint of milk
1 egg, separated

METHOD

1 Place ground rice and sugar in a basin and mix with a little milk to a paste.*
2 Boil the rest of the milk and pour over the ground rice, stirring all the time.
3 Return to the pan and, stirring constantly, bring to the boil. Simmer for 5 minutes, stirring frequently.
4 Separate egg and add yolk to pan, stirring in rapidly off the heat.
5 Beat the egg white until stiff, and fold into the mixture in the pan very carefully.

Notes: This pudding may be served straight from the pan into individual dishes, or placed in a pie dish and kept hot in the oven.

  It can be eaten hot or cold.

  If plain try it served with vitamin C blackcurrant syrup.

* To vary flavour, 1 tablespoon cocoa may be added to the ground rice and sugar when mixing to a paste.

Muesli Biscuits

Makes 18 biscuits. Keep in an airtight tin.
Oven temperature: 375°F, 190°C, gas mark 5
Cooking time: about 10–15 minutes

INGREDIENTS

4 oz. dry muesli
1 oz. brown sugar
2 oz. wholemeal flour
1½ oz. ground almonds

3 oz. margarine
1½ tablespoons clear honey
¼ teaspoon bicarbonate of
   soda

METHOD

1   Mix together the muesli, sugar, flour and almonds.
2   Melt the margarine and honey in a small saucepan.
    Remove from the heat and stir in the bicarbonate of
    soda. Add to the dry ingredients and mix well.
3   Place dessertspoons of the mixture on to a greased
    baking tray, shaping gently with the fingers if neces-
    sary, then flatten with a fork.
4   Bake at 375°F, 190°C, gas mark 5 for about 10–15
    minutes until golden. They will become firmer as they
    cool.

Tea Loaf

Made in 2 easy stages – with at least 6 hours between
Oven temperature: 350°F, 180°C, gas mark 4
Cooking time: 50–60 minutes
You will need a greased 1-lb. loaf tin or a greased 1½-pint pie
dish.

INGREDIENTS

Stage 1
2 teaspoons tea
¼ pint of boiling water
4 oz. mixed, dried, cake fruit
3 oz. caster sugar

Stage 2
1 egg, beaten
8 oz. self-raising flour,
   sieved
2 heaped tablespoons
   skimmed milk powder
1 level tablespoon
   marmalade

METHOD

Stage 1
1 Make the tea with the boiling water in a teapot or cup.
   Leave to infuse for 5 minutes. Left-over tea may be
   used instead.
2 Place the fruit and sugar in a bowl and strain the tea
   over it. Leave to stand for at least 6 hours, but preferably overnight.

Stage 2

1 To the fruit mixture add the egg, flour, milk powder
   and marmalade and mix well.

2   Turn the mixture into the prepared tin, hollow out the
    centre slightly, and bake in a moderate oven 350°F,
    180°C, gas mark 4 for about 50–60 minutes. Insert a
    skewer to make certain it is fully baked. (The skewer
    should come out clean without wet mixture sticking
    to it.)
3   Serve the tea loaf sliced thinly and spread with butter.

Liquidizer Lemonade

A pint of lemonade made from a whole lemon – in a few seconds!

INGREDIENTS

1 lemon
1 pint of cold water

2 tablespoons granulated
   sugar
4 ice cubes

METHOD

1 Wash, then top and tail the lemon, i.e., slice off the thick pith at each end.
2 Place the lemon in the liquidizer and process at medium speed for 5 seconds, just to break up the fruit.
3 Add the water, sugar and ice cubes and liquidize at high speed for 10 seconds.
4 Strain the juice into a bowl through a nylon sieve; discard the fragmented pith.
5 Keep this tangy, fresh lemonade chilled before pouring into tall glasses.

Mulled 'Cider'

A warming winter beverage. Measure with a teacup.
Serves: 2–3
Cooking time: 15 minutes

INGREDIENTS

1½ cups apple juice
¼ cup orange juice
4 teaspoons lemon juice

2 whole cloves
quarter of a stick of
   cinnamon *or* a dash of
   ground cinnamon

METHOD

1   Combine all the ingredients except the lemon juice in
    a covered saucepan, bring to the boil and then simmer
    over low heat for 15 minutes.
2   Remove the cloves and cinnamon stick. Add the
    lemon juice and serve hot.

Pastry Making

Whenever recipes in this book call for pastry,

(a) Keep to your own favourite recipe; *or*

(b) Follow the fork-mix method with soft margarine that we give in detail on page 120. You may find this easier than the usual rubbing-in method; *or*

(c) Buy ready-made pastry; *or*

(d) Make up pastry from the SHORTCRUST PASTRY MIX, details given below.

Shortcrust Pastry Mix

Uses: Sweet or savoury pies, tarts, flans, tartlets, crumble topping.

INGREDIENTS

8 oz. plain flour   2 oz. hard margarine
a pinch of salt   2 oz. lard

Note: If you make a lot of pastry dishes you may like to double these quantities.

METHOD

1   Sift together flour and salt into a mixing bowl.
2   Rub in fats until mixture resembles fine breadcrumbs.
3   Store in a tightly closed polythene bag or container in a freezer for up to 6 months; in a refrigerator for up to 3 months; or in a cool dark place below 60°F for 2–3

weeks. Take out of refrigerator 30 minutes before use. In a freezer it remains free-flow so that small quantities can be removed.

To make up shortcrust pastry

1 For a recipe calling for '4 oz. shortcrust pastry' measure out 6 oz. of mix (i.e., 4 oz. flour which is already mixed with 2 oz. fat); similarly if you need '6 oz. shortcrust pastry' you would need 9 oz. of mix (i.e., 6 oz. flour which is mixed with half its weight, 3 oz., of fat).
2 To every 6 oz. mix sprinkle in 1 tablespoon of cold water and mix to a stiff dough with a knife.
3 Turn on to a lightly floured board and knead lightly until smooth.
4 Roll out to required shape and thickness of pastry. (Bake small tarts and thin pastry cases at 400°F, 200°C, gas mark 6 for 10–15 minutes; bake larger pastry cases in a hot oven 425°F, 220°C, gas mark 7 for 20–25 minutes.)

Crumble Topping

Omit water and add sugar to the dry shortcrust pastry mix – to 6 oz. mix add 2 oz. demerara sugar. Or, instead of sugar, add a little seasoning or a few herbs for a savoury mix (see STEAK AND KIDNEY CRUMBLE, page 118).

Breadcrumbs

Fresh Breadcrumbs

Bread which is a day or so old can be turned into bread-crumbs in a blender or food processor within a few seconds. If using a Mouli-type grater, the bread needs to be slightly staler. Use for stuffings, puddings or sauces.

Quantity guide: 1 medium-thick slice from a large loaf, with the crusts removed, makes roughly ½ oz. of bread-crumbs.

Keeping guide: in a sealed polythene bag, a few days in the refrigerator and up to 6 months in the freezer.

Buttered Crumbs

Toss 5 oz. fresh breadcrumbs with 1 oz. melted butter until the fat is evenly absorbed. Spread on a baking sheet and dry out, without browning, in a cool oven at 250°F, 120°C, gas mark ½. Use for coating meat, fish or croquettes.

Keeping guide: in an air-tight container, up to 2 months in the refrigerator.

For **sweet buttered crumbs:** mix 2 oz. buttered crumbs with 1 oz. demerara sugar and heat very gently without burning for a few moments. Cool and sprinkle over desserts, e.g., SWEDISH APPLE, page 195.

Chapter 6

Some Useful Hints and Information

Weighing and Measuring

Many of the recipes in this book do not need meticulously accurate weighing. If you have kitchen scales, obviously it is better to use them and for this reason we have specified ounces. Without scales use a conical Cook's Measure or turn to the Handy Measures or Yogurt Pot Measures below. Or – more likely – continue to make your own experienced judgement, you will not go far wrong.

Handy Measures

The following table gives the approximate number of *level tablespoons* which correspond to *1 oz.*:

breadcrumbs, fresh	7
breadcrumbs, dried	6
packet crumbs	4
cheese (Cheddar, grated)	3
cocoa powder	3
cornflour, custard powder, semolina	2
dried fruit (currants, sultanas, raisins)	2
flour, unsifted	3
rice, uncooked	2
rolled oats	4
suet (packet shredded)	3
sugar (granulated, caster, demerara)	2
syrup, honey, treacle	1

8 tablespoons liquid = 5 fluid oz. = ¼ pint

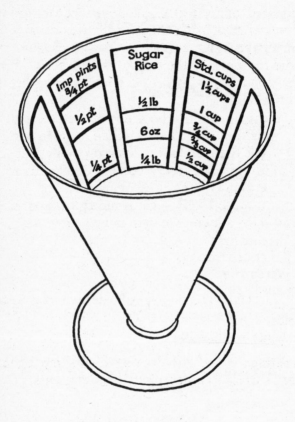

Yogurt Pot Measures

I am indebted to the Stork Cookery Service for introducing a new way of measuring without the use of scales. Using the conversion chart below, you could measure the ingredients for many of the recipes in this book *using any straight-sided empty yogurt pot that is marked 150g, 5.3 oz.* Then reckon:

1 pot = *approximately*

4 oz. white flour
3 oz. wholemeal flour
6 oz. caster or granulated sugar
4 oz. demerara or soft brown sugar
2 oz. coarsely grated cheddar cheese (loosely packed)
3½ oz. raisins
2½ oz. chopped nuts
2½ oz. desiccated coconut
2¼ oz. porridge oats
2 oz. ground almonds
7 oz. mincemeat
8 oz. golden syrup
5 fl. oz. liquid (water, milk)

When filling the pot with dry ingredients, tap it gently on the work surface in order to settle the contents.

Weights and Measures

Liquid Measures

BRITISH

1 quart	= 2 pints	= 40 fluid oz.
1 pint	= 4 gills	= 20 fl. oz.
½ pint	= 2 gills	
	or one cup	= 10 fl. oz.
¼ pint	= 8 tablespoons	= 5 fl. oz.
	1 tablespoon	= just over ½ fl. oz.
	1 dessertspoon	= ⅓ fl. oz.
	1 teaspoon	= ⅛ fl. oz.

METRIC

1 litre = 10 decilitres (dl.) = 100 centilitres (cl.) = 1000 millilitres (ml.)

Approx. equivalents

BRITISH	METRIC
1 quart	1·1 litre
1 pint	6 dl.
½ pint	3 dl.
¼ pint (1 gill)	1·5 dl.
1 tablespoon	15 ml.
1 dessertspoon	10 ml.
1 teaspoon	5 ml.

METRIC	BRITISH
1 litre	35 fl. oz.
½ litre (5 dl.)	18 fl. oz.
¼ litre (2·5 dl.)	9 fl. oz.
1 dl.	3½ fl. oz.

Solid Measures

BRITISH	METRIC
16 oz. = 1 lb.	1000 grammes (g) = 1 kilogramme (kilo)

Approximate equivalents:

METRIC	BRITISH
450 g	1 lb. (16 oz.)
225 g	½ lb. (8 oz.)
100 g	¼ lb. (4 oz.)
25 g	1 oz.

METRIC	BRITISH
1 kilo (1000 g)	2 lb. 3 oz.
½ kilo (500 g)	1 lb. 2 oz.
¼ kilo (250 g)	9 oz.
100 g	4 oz.

How to Keep Foods Fresh

Under the heading of 'Luxury Equipment' on page 267 I have said that a refrigerator is more of a necessity than a luxury e.g. small refrigerators ideal for a one- or two-person household.

It is a risk to leave, for example, raw or cooked meat or poultry, as well as many other foods, unrefrigerated because food-poisoning organisms can multiply rapidly. Quite apart from food poisoning, food that has to be thrown out because it has gone stale is a waste of money. We all know that it is not always possible to buy in quantities sufficient only for one, so there are times when left-overs have to be kept.

A refrigerator is even more essential if you make a habit of buying and cooking enough for more than one meal, keeping the rest for a later meal. Remember, stomach upsets caused by food poisoning are always unpleasant; they can be even more debilitating and dangerous if you are elderly or in a frail state of health.

The following hints are not given to encourage you to manage without a refrigerator, but I am attempting to be realistic; if you just cannot afford a refrigerator, do at least take the following simple precautions.

Keeping Foods Fresh Without a Refrigerator

Bacon

- Unpack and wrap *loosely* in foil or plastic film or greaseproof paper; or put it in a loosely covered dish. Keep it as cool as possible. Smoked bacon keeps a little longer than unsmoked or green bacon.
- Vacuum-packed bacon can be left unopened but must be

kept cold. Once opened – before the expiry-date stamp –
keep as above.
- Mild or sweetcure bacon must be kept in a refrigerator.

Bread

- A wrapped sliced loaf: open one end of wrapping to let
air in.
- An unwrapped loaf: put into a clean plastic bag, the ends
just folded over loosely.
- Clean out crumbs regularly because they soon spread
mould. If you use a plastic bag, it is not essential to have
a bread bin. But if you have a bread bin it is a good idea to
rinse it with a clean, damp cloth sprinkled with a few
drops of vinegar; then dry thoroughly. This helps to
prevent the spread of mould.
- Loaves which keep freshest longest are those enriched
with fat, gluten breads, starch-reduced loaves and malt
bread.
- To freshen loaves that have become a little stale, wrap
them in foil and heat in a hot oven at 450°F, 230°C, gas
mark 8 for 5–10 minutes. Remove from the oven and
allow to cool in the foil.
- Crusty bread and rolls can be crisped up by heating
*un*covered in a hot oven. Serve warm.

Butter, margarine and cooking fat

- In hot weather use an earthenware butter crock. Or
stand wrapped packet upright in a basin containing a
little cold water. Put it in an airy place and drape wet
butter muslin or a thin wet cloth over the top, touching
the packet and dipping into the water (see *'Milk'*).

Canned Foods

- Avoid badly dented or rusted cans, even if they are on special offer. As a rough guide, canned foods should have a shelf life as follows:-

Canned Food Storage Times

Rhubarb	9 months
Evaporated milk, cream, milk puddings:	1 year
New potatoes; blackberries; blackcurrants; gooseberries; plums; prunes; raspberries; strawberries:	1½ years
Other vegetables; other fruits; baked beans; pasta; soups; fish in sauce; ready meals; hot meat products:	2 years
Solid pack cold meat products; fish in oil:	5 years

Eggs

- Avoid buying eggs from shops where they are displayed in a sunny window. At home avoid warm, sunny storage.
- Keep eggs as cool as possible in a covered egg rack or in a container with a lid in which eggs are bought.
- Do not keep eggs near strong-smelling foods.
- Store eggs pointed end down so that when the yolk rises the airspace at the top stops it from touching the shell.

Fish

- Unwrap fish as soon as you get it home and store it, in the cool, in a loosely covered dish.

- Cook fish on the day of purchase. Even smoked fish does not keep well – only a little longer than unsmoked fish.
- Vacuum-packed fish can be left unopened but must be kept cold. Once opened – before the expiry date stamp – use immediately.

Gravy

- It is advisable not to keep gravy from one day to the next without a refrigerator.
- If you make a casserole which is enough for two days, the gravy in it must be cooled rapidly in the casserole. Next day the casserole must be re-boiled thoroughly right through to the centre.

Meat and Poultry

- Keep raw meat and poultry in the cold, not touching anything cooked, including cooked meat. This is because if germs from the raw meat are transferred by contact – or by your hands – to already cooked foods they may rapidly multiply, if left in a warm place or unrefrigerated in the kitchen.
- Unwrap meats straight away and keep in a loosely covered dish or use a flyproof dish cover.
- Cook *completely* and *thoroughly* as soon as possible. Never partly cook meat or poultry to finish cooking later.
- Always wash hands, boards and implements after touching raw meat or poultry. This is essential to avoid the spread of food-poisoning bacteria.

Milk

- Never leave milk in the sun and light; if you cannot take it in immediately, ask the milkman to place it in the shade.
- Keep milk in an airy place. Keep the untorn bottle cap on to protect it from dust and flies.
- In very hot weather use a milk cooler or put a little cold water in a basin, stand the milk bottle or carton in it and cover with wet butter muslin or a thin wet cloth dipping into the water. The evaporation from the cloth will keep the milk cool. From time to time replace the cold water in the basin. You must make sure that the muslin or cloth is kept wet.
- Never use milk which smells 'off'.

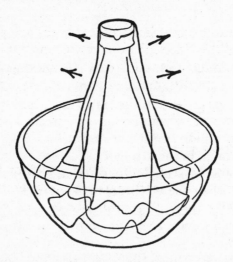

Pet foods

- Raw or uncanned pet meat should be kept separate from family foods; use different utensils and surfaces for their preparation. Wash and dry pets' dishes and utensils separately from your own.

Potatoes

- Keep potatoes in a large brown paper bag and fold the top over loosely to exclude the light.
- Put the bag of potatoes in a vegetable rack or cool corner.
- Storage in the light, especially near fluorescent light or sunlight, turns potatoes green on the outside. If only slightly green, cut off that part; if dark green, throw the whole potato away.

Salads and Green Vegetables

- In hot weather treat lettuces, cabbages and greens like this: sprinkle with a little cold water and put in a tightly covered saucepan in a cool place. Use as soon as possible while they are still fresh.

Left-overs

- If you have a refrigerator, never cool hot food in it because you will merely raise the temperature of the refrigerator.

Canned Foods

- Once a can is opened, the contents should be kept only as long as fresh foods. If you are not using the whole of the can, turn the rest out and keep it cool and covered.
- It is best not to keep an opened can of a meat product overnight without a refrigerator.

Dairy Foods
- It is unwise to keep cream cakes, trifles, milk puddings and similar desserts from one day to the next, if you do not have very cold storage conditions. If you keep them in the cold, remember to keep them covered.

Meat or Poultry
- Avoid long, slow cooling. Put the warm meat or poultry in a covered dish and run the cold tap on it. If possible, for instance with casseroles, meat cakes etc., stir the contents of the dish from time to time to encourage quick cooling. After this rapid drop in temperature store it covered (e.g., with a lid or under a flyproof dish cover) in a cold place and use within 24 hours.

Food and Nutrition

Here are some of the foods supplying a mixture of nutrients but particularly valuable for:

Vitamin A

Margarine and butter, eggs, whole milk, cream and cheeses (except those made from skimmed milk), liver and kidney, green and leafy vegetables, carrots, tomatoes, mainly yellow fleshed fruits, e.g., apricots, peaches.

Vitamin B group

Meat and bacon, liver and kidney, fish roe, flour and bread particularly wholemeal, yeast and meat extracts, milk, cheese, eggs, vegetables, fortified breakfast cereals.

Vitamin C

Vegetables, especially green leafy vegetables and potatoes, citrus fruit and juices, especially oranges, satsumas, clementines, grapefruit and lemons, blackcurrants and berry fruits, some products labelled as being fortified with vitamin C, e.g., some fruit drinks, instant mashed potato.

Vitamin D

Fatty fish, e.g., sardines, pilchards, herrings and kippers, tuna, salmon, margarine and butter, eggs, cod roe, fortified foods, e.g., some breakfast cereals. Also of prime importance: the action of sunlight on the skin.

Calcium

Milk (whole or skimmed), yogurt and cheeses, flour and bread (other than wholemeal), spinach, fish eaten with bones e.g., pilchards, sardines, whitebait, some shellfish, also drinking water in hard water areas.

Iron

Liver and kidney, meat and bacon, flour and bread, fortified breakfast cereals, green vegetables, pulses (including baked beans), dried fruit, cocoa, treacle, curry powder.

Dietary fibre

Flour and bread especially wholemeal, cereals especially wholegrain, vegetables including pulses, fruits including nuts and dried fruits.

Zinc

Meat, liver, eggs, shellfish and wholegrain cereals.

Potassium

Nearly all foods except sugars and fats.

Selenium

Only minute amounts needed – widespread availability in foods.

Gifts to Give to Yourself or to Others

The lists below are not intended to be a complete selection of kitchen equipment. We merely hope they will solve some present-giving problems and that these ideas will prevent the sometimes desperate selection of socks and sweets and shawls.

Prices range from a few pence to several pounds, but we cannot quote prices because they are so likely to change. Instead the items are divided into three groups: kitchen gadgets, equipment (some quite inexpensive) and luxury equipment.

If you want more ideas – particularly if you or your friends are disabled – send for the book *Kitchen Sense for Disabled People*, edited by Gwen Conacher, available from Haigh & Hochland, International University Booksellers, Precinct Centre, Oxford Road, Manchester, published price £8.95 plus 50p post and packing.

The Disabled Living Foundation at 380 Harrow Road, London W9 (telephone 01-289 6111) has a permanent exhibition of gadgets and equipment, with kitchen areas (including the BBC 'In Touch' kitchen for the visually handicapped). Visitors are welcome by appointment. If you are unable to visit, you could telephone or write, giving details of specific difficulties (S A E appreciated). Or write for their lists 'Household Fittings', 'Household Equipment', 'A Kitchen for the Visually Handicapped', price £1.20 each.

For left-handed equipment, write to Anything Left-handed Ltd, 65 Beak Street, London, W1 3LF, enclosing three second-class stamps for their catalogue.

Our choice of some of the equipment listed was also helped by a guided tour of the hardware department at John Lewis P L C, Oxford Street, London W1.

Kitchen gadgets

Baking parchment – a non-stick vegetable parchment which needs no greasing – for lining baking tins. Also available in rounds, squares and strips for lining bases and sides of tins, although these may be harder to find.

Bottle-top opener – a rubber cap fitting over a bottle top provides additional friction for unscrewing. A do-it-yourself alternative: wear a plastic or rubber washing-up glove to give a grip when unscrewing bottles. Also available: a milk-bottle opener.

Clamps and other securing aids to help those cooking with unsteady hands or with one hand, e.g., double suction rubber bowl for stabilizing mixing bowl; one surface adheres firmly to smooth work top when dampened, whilst the top will hold a bowl firmly. Also useful for the one-handed to dry up crockery. Inexpensive. Also available spike boards for spreading or slicing – in rigid plastic with four suction feet. Useful for the cook able to use only one hand; stabilizes meat, bread, etc. The spikes are not sharp.

Cloths – use a cellulose sponge cloth which can be boiled and is easily kept clean. Extra use: when dampened and placed under bowl or dish, helps to stabilize whilst mixing, cutting or serving food. Alternative: non-slip mats.

Egg separator which effectively separates whites from yolks.

Egg slicer and/or wedger. For easy chopping of hard-boiled eggs, choose a slicer with a double hollow which enables you to slice the egg then turn it at right angles, so that the second slice chops it.

Egg pricker – to avoid cracking eggs when boiling.

Food cover – a muslin 'umbrella' to keep flies off food.

Funnels – in easily cleaned plastic.

Glasses – choose bright coloured stems with coloured ring pattern near the top to help to prevent over-filling. Choose cup shapes with two-handled holders for easy lifting.

Grater – box-shaped for easy holding. Some have a tray to reduce spillage.

Kitchen tongs, cook's spoon and cook's fork.

Left-handed gadgets – e.g., can opener, corkscrew, pie-cutter with serrated edge, potato peeler/kitchen knife, spatula, scissors, including specially designed scissors with an easy to hold grip particularly suitable for those suffering from arthritis.

Lemon squeezer.

Lid unscrewer – an inexpensive V-shaped device for unscrewing lids, to be fixed to under-surface of shelf or worktop.

Lighter for gas stoves – ignition type which clicks whilst giving a continuous spark is safer to use than matches or tapers.

Measures – spoons and cups in either Imperial or metric

measures; a conical cook's measure (see the illustration on page 248) as another inexpensive alternative to kitchen scales; an empty yogurt pot (see weight conversions on page 249).

Milk saver – e.g., a circle of toughened glass which, when placed in saucepan, prevents milk from boiling over. It gives an audible warning when the milk nears boiling point.

Oven gloves – a length of material padded on the surface of the palm and folded over at each end to form gloves. Needs to be thick enough to prevent heat penetration but not so thick that you cannot handle hot casseroles. The connecting material between the 'gloves' lessens the danger of burning the arms above the wrist.

Pan stands.

Plate warmers with night-light or hot water could be helpful to those who eat slowly.

Potato peeler.

Scissors for kitchen use.

Slicer – (rather like a narrow long-toothed comb) spears and steadies the food while you slice between the prongs.

Spatula – flexible.

Splatter screen – a mesh to put over frying pans to avoid hot oil splashes.

Steamer basket – fits into saucepan to enable pudding basins, vegetables, etc., to be lifted out without scalding hands. Avoids over-boiled vegetables with their excessive loss of water-soluble vitamins and minerals (See the recipe on page 68).

Storage – kitchen foil, cling wrap, polythene bags.

Teaspoon tea infuser – labour-saving device for making tea for one person if you do not use teabags.

Equipment

Beaters and whisks (hand-held) – rotary beaters are designed to be used left-handed or right-handed. Electric blender Multi-practic (hand-held) – an electrically operated blade to whisk into pans or bowls for speedy purées.

Balloon whisks, see illustration, page 170. Spring whisk which can be used by either hand or by both hands together, see illustration, page 127. Coil whisk, see illustration, page 232.

Can openers, hand-held or wall-mounted; electric can openers help those with limited grip.

Chopping boards – Formica boards, dark-coloured one side, light the other, to make more visual impact for the semi-sighted; white non-porous polythene boards which do not stain, absorb juice, retain odours or blunt your knives.

Cookware – microwave cookware: check that it can also be used for conventional cooking in the oven as well as on top of the stove (gas, electric or ceramic hob) and under the grill. Invaluable for one-pan cooking to save washing up. Dishwasher proof. Look for the small soufflé dishes and oval casseroles suitable for one or two portions.

Oven-to-table porcelain – some can also be placed on a flame or electric ring if a heat diffuser is used.

Oven-to-table toughened glass – including ovenproof casseroles, soufflé dishes, pie plates and other dishes of small enough size for one or two servings.

Foil baking dishes – small sizes for one or two portions for pies, tartlets, flans, casseroles and other cooking. Suitable for freezer. Reusable.

Frying pan (electric) – now more accurately known as a multi-purpose cooker because it can be used for frying, boiling, stewing, roasting or even baking.

Kettles (non-electric) with whistle for forgetful cooks; *(electric)* – with automatic switch-off; *jug kettles* for boiling small, measured amounts. Plastic finish for cool-to-touch outside.

Knives – a range of sharp, stainless knives speeds food preparation. Victorinox has a 'Dux' knife with a blade and adjustable guide which can be set to the required thickness and pressed against the food (bread, meat, cabbage or other vegetables or fruit), so that the visually handicapped and blind can cut regular slices. Skyline has a particularly effective serrated, thin-bladed tomato knife.

A magnetic knife rack – keeps knives in view and avoids cut fingers whilst searching in drawers.

Measuring jug – heatproof glass, graduated for Imperial and metric measures. Rigid plastic, open-end handle, can facilitate gripping for those with hand impairments.

Mincer – suction-based, to stand firmly without screws or clamps on any non-porous surface such as enamel or laminated plastic.

Mouli kitchen ware – for sieving, shredding, grating, chopping, slicing and mincing. See the illustration on page 53. A large size can be stabilized on a bowl and used for puréeing soup. Use also for sieving pippy fruits.

Non-stick cake and patty tins – no need to line or grease; the contents can be tipped out easily; also *non-stick saucepans and frying pans*. When used according to instructions these are extremely easy to keep clean.

Polythene containers – with tightly fitting lids: bowls jugs, food canisters, beakers and storage boxes in various shapes, sizes and colours. Suitable for larder or freezer.

Pressure cooker – for speedy, economical and nourishing cooking.

Saucepans, including small two-pint size with well-fitting lid. Can be found with twin handles for easy lifting.

Choose from aluminium, stainless steel or enamel. Now also made in attractive see-through transparent glass or tough glass ceramic with coloured designs.

Scales for weighing ingredients – compact jug scales; spring-balance scales with wide, easily read markings (Braille is available); scales with accurate weights both Imperial and metric; digital scales, expensive but very accurate.

Slow-cooking pots – economical on fuel. The meal is left cooking to be eaten later in the day.

Space savers – plastic covered wire trays for stacking china in a small space. Also space-saving baskets, drawers and shelves.

Toasters – latest pop-up electric versions adapt to thickness and freshness of bread or crumpets. For toasters which are cool to the touch, choose plastic outside.

Sandwich toasters (electric – shaped to seal in plenty of filling for savoury or sweet snacks (see page 21).

Timer – set the clock alarm to ring as a reminder. If you make cakes or casseroles, look for a two-hour timer.

Trays – including special designs for one handed lifting.

Vegetable chopper – the knives rotate automatically when the plunger is pushed rapidly up and down into the perspex cage. Use it for onions without tears. Also for speedy chopping of other vegetables and salads, fruits and nuts. Try it for MUSHROOM SOUP, page 51.

Luxury equipment

Automatic tea-maker.
Dish washer – a wonderful family Golden Wedding present.
Electric beater, hand held. Try with soufflés needing to be whisked over hot water.
Food mixers and processors:
  (a) beaters and bowl – takes the muscle out of cake making and other baking.
  (b) blender or liquidizer – chops, grinds, mixes and purées. It will grate breadcrumbs or make home-made mayonnaise in a few seconds. Try also LIQUIDIZER LEMONADE, page 242.
  (c) food processor – for slicing, shredding, chopping, puréeing without effort. Grates or slices hard vegetables such as carrots in a few seconds. Try with CARROT AND ORANGE SOUP, page 52.
Freezer – enables you to shop less frequently if you wish; to cook in larger quantities, eat one portion and freeze the rest; to buy foods cheaper in season or larger economy sizes to use later, a little at a time; to store ready-bought frozen foods and ice. (See basic freezer stores, page 218.) *Fridge-freezers* are now popular and most refrigerators have an ice-making compartment for short term storage of frozen food.
Fryer – deep fat. Small size, compact fryers now available, with built-in safety precautions.
Microwave cookers – becoming extremely popular. Can cook in a fraction of the conventional time with fuel economy. Cookers are generally supplied with full instructions and recipe booklets. I have therefore not given specific recipes for microwaves, but many of the recipes in

this book could easily be adapted to your microwave cooking.

Refrigerator – (although it could be argued that, for hygienic short-term storage of foods, this is more of a necessity than a luxury).

Table-top cookers – portable and small enough to take with you if you move accommodation.

Trolleys – some will give partial support as you push, or provide extra storage space.

Index